Tying Flies with CDC

The Fisherman's Miracle Feather

Leon Links

STACKPOLE
BOOKS

Tying Flies with CDC
The Fisherman's Miracle Feather

First published in the USA by **Stackpole Books, Mechanicsburg** in 2002
Published originally in the UK by **Merlin Unwin Books, Ludlow** in 2002

Copyright 2002

U.S. edition published in 2002 by
STACKPOLE BOOKS
5067 Ritter Road
Mechanicsburg, PA 17055
www.stackpolebooks.com

Library of Congress Cataloging-in-Publication Data
CIP data is on file with the Library of Congress.

Designed by **think : graphic design**, Ludlow, UK.
Printed and bound in China

First Edition

ISBN 0-8117-00399-9

For Jenny and Christa

Contents

Acknowledgements

Publishing a book on CDC has always been a dream to me. Now this has turned into a reality, with the help of numerous people to whom I owe many thanks:

Marjan Fratnik for being my best friend and guide in many aspects, for his encouragement and for sharing his immense knowledge of flies and feathers;

Marc Petitjean for writing the preface and for being such a wonderful host, for giving support and sharing his knowledge of flies and feathers;

Henk Baan for his enthusiasm, good ideas and patience while reading and commenting on my texts;

Karen and Merlin Unwin for believing in the project, for their advice and support during the writing process;

Tony Deacon for editing my script;

John Roberts for his help and encouragement, and for writing the foreword;

Ina and Hans van Klinken for their friendship over the years, for their inspiration, their flies and for introducing and guiding me in the land of small, lousy mosquitoes and large grayling;

Rudy van Duijnhoven for his pictures and indispensable help while shooting the pictures of tying instructions and fly plates;

Paolo Jaia for his flies and putting me in touch with tiers in Italy;

Elie Beerten for his flies and putting me in touch with tiers in England;

Nicolas Ragonneau for his flies and putting me in touch with the French tiers;

Tetsumi Himeno for introducing me to the Japanese tiers

Theo Bakelaar, Mitsugu Bizen, Philippe Boisson, Henri Bresson, Paul Canning, Patrick Daniels, Jean-Paul Dessaigne, Marco Feliciani, Simon Gawesworth, Gigi Goldoni, Bonnie and René Harrop, Preben Torp Jacobsen, Leon Janssen, Hans Kievits, Gerhard Laible, Hugo Martel, Didier Martenet, Marvin Nolte, Dr. J.P. Pequegnot, Clive Perkins, Charles Richter, Antonio Rinaldin, Ryo Shimazaki, Nori Tashiro, Jean-Louis Teyssié, Bas Verschoor, Louis Veya, Piet Weeda – for contributing their ideas, flies, words and pictures.

And to many others who have also contributed to this book with their ideas, flies and pictures. Alas they cannot all feature in these pages but they have been important nevertheless and I thank them for their help and kindness.

Leon Links

I have rarely come across anyone who researches a subject as thoroughly as Leon Links and I know from my discussions with him how he has included in this book only a proportion of the material gathered. Leon has met, discussed and fished with most of the tyers featured in this book. I doubt whether anyone knows this material better and how the patterns are fished to get the best out of them. Leon is an expert at the tying vice, especially with CDC, and for many seasons I have enjoyed considerable success with the patterns he has sent me to try out. He is a skilled flytyer but also an accomplished and thoughtful fisherman – a rare combination which means that he writes with particular authority and insight. This is an immensely useful book about a subject which for a long time has been deserving of a comprehensive exposition in English.

Cul de canard, or CDC, feathers have changed irrevocably the way the modern flytyer approaches the challenge of imitating the natural fly. I might even suggest that the uniqueness of certain aspects of the feather makes it more indispensable than any other tying material. This book shows that CDC feathers may be used for the tying of tails, bodies, wings and legs of an insect as no other single material may. Their versatility, and therefore their use to an enterprising tyer, is unmatched. But CDC feathers are more than just an adaptable material for the tyer; they have inherent qualities that make the artificial fly look alive. Imitation of a natural nymph or fly is relatively easy to achieve with the wide range of materials currently on offer – but how many materials suggest life and movement within the material itself? By careful use of CDC your imitation fly will have wings that flutter, legs that tremble and gills that move within the current.

Leon Links shows in this book how CDC feathers have enabled flytying to take a large step forward. How the CDC flytyer has come a little closer to achieving that most elusive of goals – the imitation of life itself.

John Roberts
York, July 2002

When I designed my first CDC dry fly patterns, I never expected that this fabulous material was to conquer the entire planet a few decades later! The real potential of CDC as a flytying material only became apparent to me during my flyfishing experiments on the river.

In the 1980s very few anglers could accept the idea that nymphs, streamers and salmon flies could consist of 100% CDC. I well remember an article published in the fishing press at that time in which I was roundly blamed for having created a series of nymphs and streamers made exclusively out of Cul de Canard feathers! CDC was, of course, pre-eminently a material for dry flies.

It took many years before the Swiss tradition of using CDC in all manner of ways came to be recognised and copied.

CDC has certainly risen to fame today but it is, paradoxically, still not very well understood, since the majority of flydressers only use a limited number of tying techniques.

I believe that in the years to come we will see numerous further developments due to the plasticity of tying materials – especially of a versatile material like CDC – and this offers an infinite number of possibilities to the tyer.

It is not a coincidence that CDC has seduced the entire flyfishing world!

Leon Links has produced the first international and comprehensive book on the subject. It is both historical (tracing the early days of CDC) as well as practical (full of tips for flytyers and with a considerable number of step-by-step sequences).

This is a remarkable reference book, the product of a great deal of hard work done with patience and passion.

Bravo Leon – and thanks!

Marc Petitjean
Fribourg, July 2002

This book is devoted to the fascinating subject of tying and fishing with CDC flies. In recent years, CDC has become of major importance in modern flyfishing and an ever-increasing number of flytyers around the world are discovering the usefulness and potential of this extraordinary material. This book starts with a little history of the use of CDC feathers in flytying, then goes on to give more detailed information about the material, the patterns that can be tied with it and some new ideas for its application in flytying.

The first CDC flies were tied back in the 1920s, but it wasn't until the 1980s that real international interest in the material was stimulated when the Slovenian, Marjan Fratnik, introduced his revolutionary F Fly. In the second half of the 1980s, the German flytyer, Gerhard Laible, developed new ways of tying with CDC. Then, in the late 1980s, Marc Petitjean from Switzerland took things still further with some wonderful techniques and fly patterns. It was these three, above all, whose work with CDC stimulated such renewal and enrichment of flytying and flyfishing. The increasing global reputation of CDC in the 1990s was certainly largely down to them. For this reason, I felt that these pioneers deserved individual chapters of their own. As time has passed, many creative tyers have devised CDC patterns worthy of attention. I am extremely happy, therefore, that CDC addicts from all over the world have agreed to contribute to this book by sending me their flies and generously supplying me with information.

In the relevant chapters there are tying instructions of patterns showing the most important techniques. Tying with CDC is not actually very difficult, but one must learn to handle the material and know a few tricks. I have selected a number of attractive and effective flies and tied them as closely as possible to the originals, employing authentic materials and using the proper techniques. If I haven't succeeded completely in this, I hope the originators will forgive me.

Whether or not this book is your first introduction to tying flies with CDC, I hope it will provide some useful information and stimulate your own experiments with this fascinating material. A word of warning though: tying CDC flies and fishing with them is extremely addictive!

Leon Links
Zoetermeer, Holland
July 2002

In the late 1950s, the Frenchman Henri Bresson coined the name 'Cul de Canard' (duck's bum) for his fly pattern tied with duck's preen gland feathers. This title, with its slightly racy connotation, was favourably received and maybe even contributed to the reputation of the fly. Some thirty years later, Anglo-Americans adopted the abbreviation CDC, possibly because some had difficulty in pronouncing the original French. For whatever reason, the new appellation has stuck and the term CDC has become almost universal. A few die-hard Europeans stick to 'Cul de Canard', or even simply the abbreviated form 'Cul'.

The Petit Voilier, tied by Marc Petitjean

Why CDC?

Personally, I am firmly of the view that the use of CDC represents the single most important development in flytying in the last few decades, both for river and still water flyfishing. As a material, CDC has truly exceptional qualities and - perhaps uniquely - has allowed the flytyer to re-interpret many of the standard patterns of the past.

When I speak of a CDC pattern, I refer to one where the fly is principally constructed with the material, or where CDC fibres constitute a significant component in the dressing and contribute to one or more of its 'triggers'. I define 'trigger' as any feature of an artificial which provokes a taking response by the fish. It can include the shape of the body; presence of wings, legs and tails; colour; translucency; position of the fly on or in the water; and behaviour.

Insects crawl, swim and flutter, so our artificial imitations need to emulate these movements in order to attract the fish. One of the principal virtues of CDC is that it provides this suggestion of liveliness. It only needs a breath of air to move the CDC element incorporated into a floating fly. Similarly, in a sub-surface pattern, the slightest movement in the water causes CDC fibres to wave seductively and imitate the natural insect's own movements.

CDC is extremely light. Provided a cast is made with some finesse, a CDC fly seems to glide smoothly through the air during the delivery, then slow down and 'open up' again before alighting quietly on the surface. There is no doubt about it: CDC flies can be presented with great delicacy and seem to frighten the fish less. Moreover, instead of floating on pricking hackle points (as in a conventional dry fly) the CDC fibres rest on the surface like little insect feet, thus giving a soft and natural silhouette.

CDC flies have low air resistance. The pliable fibres give the fly an aerodynamic shape during flight, a substantial plus-point when fishing larger patterns. CDC diminishes the irritating spinning of the fly and kinking of the leader that often occurs with some other kinds of artificial fly construction. This softness of CDC appears to have another advantage. It seems that fish are less ready to eject a soft CDC pattern than the harder, more 'prickly' dressings of conventional flies. Whatever the reason, there appears to be a higher ratio of positive hook-ups to missed strikes when using CDC flies.

The 'natural' colour shades of CDC and the translucency of the material seem to be important features. They give the fly a gauzy, transparent air about them. Many times I have noticed that opaquely solid-looking, conventional artificials were ignored, while transparent CDC flies have been accepted more readily. Mayflies, especially, have that fragility and translucence that CDC seems to imitate so convincingly.

CDC flies are buoyant, when handled with care, but even they cannot defy the laws of physics. Clumsy casting and poor fishing techniques will defeat even CDC's admirable properties. CDC dry flies and semi dry flies call for subtle casting and presentation. They have to be fished carefully and picked off the surface delicately in order for the material to give of its best. Here, as in any sphere of activity, practice makes perfect.

The Dessoubre, one of France's most beautiful – and difficult – flyfishing rivers. *Leon Janssen*

Not only the F Fly

I often meet people whose great enthusiasm for the virtues of CDC is founded solely on their experience with F Flies, or similar patterns. This doesn't surprise me at all because Marjan Fratnik's well-known pattern is easy to tie and very effective indeed.

Simon Gawesworth, a member of the England International Fly Fishing Team, had something interesting to say on this subject in *the Journal of the Grayling Society*, Autumn 1999. 'The best dry fly anglers in the world (as a team) are the French. It doesn't matter if the quarry are the wild brown trout of the English and French classic rivers, the rainbows and cut-throats of America (where they again won the gold medal), or grayling from the streams of Central Europe – they are absolute masters with the dry fly and it is their attention to all the minutest details that makes them so good.'

In the same article he writes: 'The number one fly, though, for choice has to be the cul de canard. In the World Championships last year I was shown one of the fly boxes of Jean Astier. He produced the remarkable feat of catching 46 measurable (over eight inch) grayling in three hours, fishing on one stretch of river – all on a size 20 cul de canard. His box contained dozens of cul de canard flies, all tied on 18s, 20s and 22s.'

All of them were F Fly-like patterns, tied with various body colours and materials. I am neither surprised by Gawesworth's admiration for French dry flyfishing, nor by the appreciation of this French competitor for F Flies. The French are true masters of the dry fly, because they have to deal with difficult fishing conditions. Their home rivers have wonderful hatches of insects, but there are relatively few fish because of the fishing pressure and because, traditionally, most of the fish that are caught are killed for the table. As far back as 1939, Tony Burnand and Charles Ritz wrote in their book *A la Mouche* '...fishing suffers and dies in France because of a lack of sportsmanship of fishermen...' Things are somewhat different today in France and there are widespread method restrictions and regulations designed to improve stocks. Some rivers are 'dry fly only', so anglers simply have to be good dry fly fishers.

CDC patterns like the F Fly have been popular in France for a considerable time. Around 1985 a fly called the *Petit Voilier*, with a Fratnik-style wing, was commercially produced and sold. A notable feature of this pattern is that, in order to save cost, only one CDC feather was used. The feather is tied in backwards over the body, the tip is then folded back to form the wing and tied off.

It would seem, then, that while many people use F Flies and similar patterns, they are often unaware of the many other uses of CDC. We shall look at some of the many other ways in which CDC can be used in a wide variety of attractive and effective patterns. It is important to note that the use of CDC is not restricted to dry flies. In the last decade or so the use of CDC in nymphs and streamers has gradually caught on. This has been due mainly to the inventiveness of that great proponent of CDC, the Swiss specialist, Marc Petitjean.

Marc Petitjean's quest to identify the first tyers of CDC flies

Three variations of the Moustique du Jura showing different body colours, tied by the Swiss flytyer, Louis Veya.

Marc Petitjean lives in the part of Europe where CDC flies almost certainly first appeared. He has devoted no small effort in trying to discover the actual origins of CDC use in flytying. Who was the genius to have discovered the benefits of duck preen gland feathers and hit upon the idea of using them in fly patterns? And when exactly were the very first CDC flies tied?

When Marc first embarked on his researches, clear and reliable information seemed to be lacking. Even an expert on French flies, Dr. Jean-Paul Pequegnot, from Besançon, is not sure. In his famous *L'Art de la Pêche à la Mouche Sèche* (1996), Pequegnot states that in the 1940s (or even earlier) a Swiss fisherman from Vallorbe - a small Swiss town near Pontarlier in France, but on the Swiss side of the River Doubs - discovered the special attraction of a fly tied with the preen gland feathers of a duck.

Eventually, Petitjean identified two men - Charles Bickel and Maximilien Joset - who were almost certainly tying CDC flies in the 1920s. It was probably one of these two who deserves the credit for the first use of CDC, but which of them it was is now likely to remain a mystery. Surely, one must have copied the other, since it seems highly unlikely that two flytyers living in the same region should independently have come up with something as unusual as using CDC at more-or-less the same time. One problem with this theory, however, is that Bickel and Joset lived about 100 km apart in a mountainous area with fairly poor road communications. Contact between the two would have been difficult, but can't of course be ruled out.

Louis Veya

At Courfaivre, in the northern part of the Swiss Jura, Marc Petitjean came across an old flytyer by the name of Louis Veya. Veya told him that he had learned to tie the 'Moustiques' - as they were called in this part of the Jura - a very long time ago from a Maximilien Joset. Joset had been a farmer and woodcutter from the same village as Veya and was reputed to be an outstanding fisherman and flytyer. According to Veya, Joset first tied his Moustiques in the 1920s, though it was about 1935 that he (Veya) first saw Joset tying them. Veya was very young at the time and it wasn't until some years later, in 1942, that he became interested in tying flies himself and learned the techniques.

Louis Veya, one of the earliest exponents of CDC flytying, holding a prized mallard drake. He learned much about CDC from Maximilien Joset. *Charles Richter*

Max Joset tied the original Moustiques with a collar hackle of CDC feathers and a body of silk. In Marc Petitjean's view these archetypal CDC flies were used as dry flies fished in the surface film. With their floating CDC hackles and sinking bodies, they give a good impression of emerging insects. Along with the superb 'soft hackle' action of the CDC fibres, we can imagine what excellent fish catchers these Moustiques must have been. Indeed, they still are today.

Today, Louis Veya still ties his flies pretty much as he first learned from Max Joset. Over the course of time he added tails of cock hackle fibres and replaced the body silk with Swiss Straw (Raffene), because it darkens less when wet.

A unique moment in the summer of 1996 in which four of the great CDC flytyers of recent times met up to fish on the French rivers Loue and Doubs. The meeting was arranged by Marc Petitjean and in the picture (from right to left) are: Louis Veya, Marjan Fratnik, Gerhard Laible, Marc Petitjean and unknown friend. *Charles Richter*

The Courfaivre Moustiques gained a certain fame and, with a growing demand for them after the war, Veya started tying them professionally for well-known firms in Geneva and Basel.

To Vallorbe

Marc Petitjean's next step was some 100 kilometres south to Vallorbe, as some of the early CDC flies were known as 'Mouches de Vallorbe'. By a stroke of luck, Petitjean learned from a Vallorbe woman that her uncle, Charles Bickel, had tied flies with duck's preen gland feathers as early as the 1920s. He had even given up his job in the local file factory to become a professional flytyer, eventually employing a dozen people in his studio. Through this fortuitous contact, Petitjean obtained a unique collection of original 'Bickel' flies. Charles Bickel's niece gave him several series of flies mounted on old paper display sheets. These included wet flies, grayling flies, and two series of CDC flies. One of these was a wonderful display of 24 flies (size 16), with texts in both French and German:

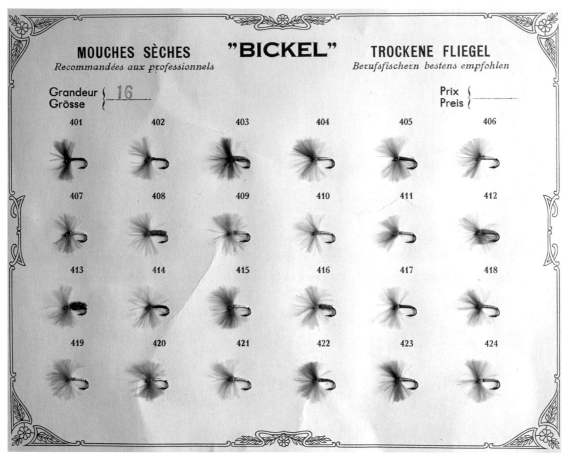

A plate advertising Charles Bickel's famous flies. Each one an exercise in simplicity and economy.

Questions remain

So what prompted Maximilien Joset and Charles Bickel to use duck preen gland feathers in their flies and at more-or-less the same time? Did they experiment much to improve their flies, intended for the shy and fastidious trout and grayling of the Jura's crystal clear streams? We can only guess.

Maximilien Joset, a farmer and woodcutter from the northern Swiss Jura, was one of the first people known to have seriously tie flies using CDC.

18

Maximilien Joset and Charles Bickel are no longer with us. The latter died in 1945. Whilst it is not possible to get all the answers to our questions, we have the account of Louis Veya and the information supplied by Charles Bickel's niece. And we have some of Bickel's actual flies. The picture is not complete, but at least we have some information about the early history of CDC flies.

MOUSTIQUE

Hook:	TMC 5230, size 14–20
Thread:	Black 8/0
Tail:	Springy cock hackle fibres
Body:	Pearsall's Marabou floss silk, colours to match natural mayflies
Rib:	Pearsall's Marabou floss silk
Hackle:	One grey-brown CDC feather, medium size, with a supple stem

1. Mount the thread some way behind the eye and wind a foundation of touching turns back to the hook bend. Tie in some cock hackle fibres for the tail and wind the thread back to the shoulder.

2. Back at the shoulder, tie in two strands of floss of contrasting colours. Wind the strand used for the main body colour (over the ribbing strand) in touching turns down to the tail and back.

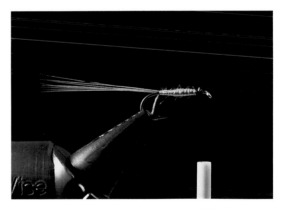

3. For a conical shaped body, wind the body floss back again three quarters down the body and back. Then, once again, this time half way down the body and back to the shoulder. Lock in the body floss with a few turns of thread and clip away the surplus.

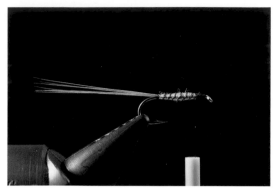

4. Firmly twist the ribbing strand and wind it forward, over the floss body, in even turns. Tie in and clip away the surplus.

5. Smooth back all the fibres of the selected CDC feather. Tie it in by the tip, on top of the shank, just in front of the body with its concave side facing the hook shank.

6. Bring the thread to the hook eye and wind the feather carefully. Four or five turns are sufficient. Try to avoid trapping any fibres by smoothing them backwards while winding the feather.

7. Secure the CDC stem with turns of thread (not too close to the eye), clip off the waste and form a neat head. Whip finish and tie off. Finish the fly by pulling the fibres forward and trimming them to desired length.

The use of CDC flies seems to have been restricted to the Swiss Jura mountain area in the 1920s and 1930s. After World War II, the use of CDC patterns spread first to the neighbouring French Jura and then further afield. Charles Bickel's studio continued producing flies and, according to Louis Veya, interest in CDC increased in this period.

In his *L'Art de la Pêche à la Mouche Sèche*, Dr. Jean-Paul Pequegnot states that by 1953, when he started flyfishing, Swiss fishermen at Goumois (a small French town on the Doubs) were regularly using CDC flies. Indeed, Pequegnot insists that some of the very first fish he caught were on CDC flies that he had bought on the banks of the Doubs. If their use on the Doubs was common by the early 1950s, it is quite possible that CDC flies were being used by French anglers even before the war.

Henri Bresson

In the 1950s, while the Swiss tended to stick with their traditional 'Moustique' patterns, it seems that the French were starting to develop their own variations.

By the late 1950s, the celebrated French professional flydresser, Henri Bresson, born in 1924 in Vesoul, came out with his 'Cul de Canard'. Its simple construction and cheeky name added to CDC's international popularity.

Bresson's Cul de Canard is very similar to the Swiss Moustique without a tail, but its CDC hackle is tied in backwards to suggest the silhouette of a floating mayfly or an emerging nymph. Together with his famous Peute, Tricolor and Sauvage, Bresson considers the Cul de Canard to be amongst his favourites.

Henri Bresson, who coined the term 'Cul de Canard' for the fly which he made entirely out of duck's pleen gland feathers. Pictured here on a trip he made to the Vosges region in France in 1999. *Fred Gimenez*

Aimé Devaux

Another professional flytyer to develop CDC his own way was Aimé Devaux, born in Champagnole in 1917. Devaux became well-known for his beautifully tied dry flies, which are hallmarked by a number of characteristic features. Many are double hackled, with the fibres of the rear hackle tied to press forward through the rearward pointing fibres of the front hackle. These crossed hackles were intended to increase floatation by presenting a larger amount of hackle fibres resting on the surface than in conventionally tied flies. Devaux flies were usually tied on hooks one size smaller than for a conventional fly of the same overall size. Tails are slightly spread cock feather fibres. In the 1970s, Devaux offered a variation to some of his best patterns, replacing the front hackle with a collar of CDC fibres.

Variations on a twig: CDC flies with different coloured bodies tied by Henri Bresson.

The Devaux CDC fly

MOUSTIQUE 'DEVAUX'

Hook:	TMC 5230, size 12–18
Thread:	Black 8/0
Tail:	Springy cock fibres
Body:	Pearsall's Marabou floss silk
Rib:	Pearsall's Marabou floss silk
Hackle:	Two khaki CDC feathers medium size, with supple stems, and one long brown partridge feather

1. Run a foundation of thread down the shank and tie in the bunch of cock hackle fibres for the tail.

2. Tie in the partridge feather halfway along the shank, with the concave side facing away from the shank. Tie in one CDC feather between the partridge feather and the hook eye and another CDC feather just behind the hook eye.

3. Leave the tying thread hanging where the second CDC feather is tied in and wind the first CDC hackle backwards towards the hanging thread and tie off. Clip off the tip. Wind the second CDC feather towards the partridge feather and finish it as for the first CDC feather.

4. Wind the partridge feather in close turns, tight against the CDC hackle. Three or four turns will do. Groom the partridge fibres forward and wind several turns of thread over the base of the fibres, so that the construction looks like an umbrella blown inside out by the wind.

5. Tie in the ribbing and body silk just behind the hackle. Tie off the tying thread.

6. Wind a slim conical body with the silk and tie in a small monofilament loop just behind the hackle.

Bring the body floss back by a few turns some millimetres from the hackle and let it hang under tension. Twist the ribbing silk to tighten the strand and wind an even ribbing forwards and secure it with turns of the body floss. Finally, wind the body floss forwards towards the monofilament 'whipping' loop again and push the end of the floss through the monofilament loop. Pull the loop back carefully until you feel resistance. Clip off the remaining silk and pull the loop completely under and out of the body.

7. Wind a head, whip finish and cut the fibres to desired length.

Dr. Jean-Paul Pequegnot

Several books and many patterns have earned Jean-Paul Pequegnot a reputation as one of France's most respected flyfishing authorities. One of his favourite patterns is the Assassine, a high floating dry fly with a sparsely palmered grey cock body hackle and a partridge front hackle. It is a deadly fly, especially during hatches of *Ephemera danica*. For particularly difficult fish, Pequegnot uses a version tied with a CDC front hackle. He doesn't use this variation regularly, though, because of its serious defect of becoming waterlogged and difficult to dry. Nevertheless, he considers this a minor drawback when dealing with very fickle trout and grayling.

CDC ASSASSINE

Hook:	TMC 5230, size 10–18
Thread:	Uni Thread 8/0 Yellow
Body:	Tying thread
Tail:	Hackle tip
Hackle:	One CDC feather with supple stem and one light blue dun cock hackle

1. Run the tying thread down the shank, then back to a position three-quarters down the shank. Tie in the cock hackle by the stem, concave side facing away from the shank. Take the thread back to the eye of the hook and tie in the CDC feather in same way. Snip off the waste CDC feather stem and form a neat head.

2. Bring the thread back to where the cock hackle is tied in. Now, wind the CDC feather backwards towards the thread point, taking care not to trap the fibres. Stop winding the CDC where the cock hackle is mounted. Tie off the CDC with three wraps of thread.

3. Snip off the remaining tip of the CDC feather, then wind the cock hackle towards the rear of the hook shank. Leave the tip of the feather for a tail. Wind the thread carefully through the cock hackle fibres. Secure the hackle tip tail with a few turns and whip finish. If necessary, lacquer the thread before whip finishing.

Notwithstanding its early beginnings, it wasn't until the 1970s that international interest in CDC really started to take off, stimulated by a few books and a number of magazine articles. Jules Rindlisbacher from Bern, Switzerland, was amongst the first to write on CDC flies in this more recent wave of interest. In 1970, in his book, *Der Praktische Fliegenfischer*, he described the 'Entenhechelfliege' - the traditional CDC fly - which he appears to have been using for some time. Rindlisbacher attempted to explain the differences between CDC patterns and other flies. He averred that the softer silhouette, without hackle tips pricking through the film, was one of the main reasons that CDC flies were so effective, especially in the daytime.

Their characteristics and uses

CDC feathers surround the preen glands of many water birds. The gland is located centrally on the lower back of the bird, and forward of the tail, roughly where the birds wingtips meet when folded and at rest. The gland produces an oil, with which the bird waterproofs its feathers. The oil that is secreted from the preen gland is stored in the 'nipple plumes', the tiny feathers covering the gland. From this store, the bird anoints its bill with the oil, which is transferred to other plumage during 'preening'.

This regular care and maintenance that the bird gives its feathers by grooming them with its oily bill protects the duck's body against cold and water and raises buoyancy. 'Like water off a duck's back' is not merely an expression.

In fact, most water birds have preen gland feathers that possess similar qualities to those of ducks. It is, however, the preen gland feathers from ducks that flytyers have found to be most generally useful and readily available.

Quality

As with all natural flytying materials, CDC has variable characteristics. Every duck species has slightly different feathers, with variations in size, colour and structure. The age of the individual also plays a part: younger birds and smaller species have smaller feathers. Wild mallards have preen gland feathers with an average size of about 30mm and some larger feathers of over 40mm. The structure of wild mallards' preen gland feathers is rather fine.

CDC feathers come in a great range of sizes, the ones in this picture range from 7cm (top left) to 1.5cm (bottom right).

Many domesticated ducks, by contrast, have larger and somewhat denser preen gland feathers. This applies especially to older birds. Preen gland feathers from geese and swans are also sold for flytying.

Quality is a relative notion, however. The appropriateness of any particular feather depends largely on its intended use. Each CDC tying technique and CDC pattern requires the right feather for the job. Shape, size and colour, density of the fibres and thickness of the stem will determine the feather's applicability. Clearly, the choice of colour should match that of the natural insect that the tyer is trying to imitate.

Long CDC feathers, such as those supplied by Marc Petitjean, are appropriate for almost every technique and for tying larger patterns, whereas the smaller feathers can only be used for smaller flies. The waste fluff that is left over from any sized preen gland feather can be used for CDC dubbing.

My selection of feathers for different techniques is as follows:

Hackling

Feathers with a slender, supple stem, or the top part of long feathers. Plumes with thick stems do not hackle easily and tend to create lumps. For a CDC hackle, there needs to be a good number and density of fibres on the feather and these should be straight and pliable. For hackling I avoid plumes with weak, fluffy fibres.

Feathers used whole

Feathers that are tied in whole, or in part (without winding, etc.), should have straight stems. A serious curve or twist in the stem makes it hard to work with. The feather should be symmetrical, with the fibres on both sides of the stem of the same length.

Fibres used in bunches

Marc Petitjean uses bunches of fibres in many of his patterns. It is far easier to pick fibres to be tied in in bunches from the larger feathers in the 30mm–50mm size range.

For spinning loop techniques

As in the previous case, it is easier to obtain fibres for spinning loop techniques from medium to long feathers (30mm-50mm), such as those supplied by Marc Petitjean. One generally needs a great many fibres for these techniques and trying to work with smaller feathers is too troublesome and fiddly. For these techniques, stem quality is irrelevant as the stems aren't used at all.

Dubbing

There are different ways to obtain CDC dubbing. One can simply pull the fibres from the quill and use that. The most popular method is to use an electric coffee mill. The longer you 'mill' your fibres, the finer the dubbing will be. Colours can be mixed and blended by this method and almost any CDC scraps can be put to use.

Marc Petitjean-style bodies

In some of his patterns, Marc Petitjean forms a body of CDC by winding a twisted feather around the hook shank, starting with the tip of the feather tied in near the bend of the hook. Long feathers (30mm-50mm) are necessary for this purpose.

Features of CDC

CDC is a delicate natural material that combines unique qualities. Few other materials are quite so versatile for both dry and subsurface patterns.

Important characteristics of CDC are its softness, which gives a 'natural' action in the water and allows patterns tied with material to be cast easily.

The structure of CDC feathers. *Photos by Jean-Louis Teyssié*

CDC has a nice translucency and the commonly occurring natural colours are well suited to imitative flytying. Of all its characteristics, however, it is the inherent buoyancy of CDC that first comes to mind. It is also, perhaps, the least well understood. CDC is not possessed of magic. It cannot suspend the laws of physics. A CDC fly can be drowned and difficult to refloat, as any other dry fly, especially the more delicately constructed patterns. Nevertheless, a well-tied and properly designed CDC pattern can be a wonderful floater. When constructing floating flies of CDC, there are some important points to remember.

CDC is one of the lightest tying materials. The more CDC we use, the better the fly will float. Hooks, therefore, should be as light as possible in order to make the most of CDC's natural buoyancy.

CDC is impregnated with preen gland oil which waterproofs the feather and is a crucial element in the buoyancy of the plumage. Washing and dyeing tends to remove the oil from the feathers, though special dyeing techniques have been developed to mitigate this. The less that CDC feathers are handled during fishing, the longer they will retain their oil.

The actual feather structure of CDC is also an important contributor to its buoyancy. The individual plumules tend to stay apart, rather than clod together. Coupled with its hydrophobic coating of the oil, the CDC feather tends to trap bubbles of air. It is this that makes a CDC fly pop up again when it is pulled under water.

Colours and dyeing

The natural colours of CDC are grey, black, white and brown and some plumes have spotted or mottled coloration. This is fortuitous, since these are realistic imitative colours for many insects. The grey feathers of wild mallards are most common and come in all shades from white to almost black. The brown feathers also have a great colour range, from pale khaki to dark chocolate brown.

CDC flies have rather dull colours, but they are easy to spot in daylight while fishing. Surprisingly, perhaps, the grey feathers show up very well. When the light fails at dusk, other colours come in useful. Depending on the fisherman's position and the direction the light is coming from, black or white flies are more visible. Natural colours are used mostly in imitative flies, but brighter colours such as red, yellow and blue are sometimes needed in attractor patterns.

Dyeing CDC feathers has always been problematic, because of the inherent delicacy of the material. The high temperatures necessary for a normal dyeing process tend to damage CDC. Nowadays, however, dyed CDC feathers of good quality are commercially available. Marc Petitjean's collection contains feathers of natural shades and many attractive dyed colours. Some years ago, Petitjean developed a special cold dyeing

process that preserves the condition of the feathers. The process does not remove the preen gland oil and the fine structure of the plumage remains intact. Although Petitjean is secretive about his own process, acceptable methods of dying CDC have been made available from other sources.

I first started to become interested in dyeing CDC feathers for myself after Marjan Fratnik told me about the techniques he used. The procedure is as follows: dissolve Veniard dyes in cold water. The more dye you take the more intense and less transparent the result. Immerse the feathers in the dye bath and leave them there for at least 15 days. After this period of immersion, add two spoonfuls of wine vinegar. Carefully heating the dye solution will speed up the process, but be sure the feathers don't become too hot! After rinsing in cold water, the dyed feathers can be patted dry with paper towel and left to dry fully.

If you want to be sure of the final result only white feathers should be used. With other natural shades you never know exactly what the outcome will be.

An old method of dyeing insect-like yellow and olive colours is to use picric acid (trinitrophenol). However, the chemical is hard to obtain in liquid or powder form since it is rather unstable and can be explosive. Picric must be dissolved in alcohol or water, but the latter is better as it does not remove the preening oil. I have found that adding small amounts of Veniard dyes to a picric solution can improve the result.

Laying hands on CDC

Until the mid 1980s CDC feathers were hard to obtain from flytying suppliers. Today there is plenty of it about. Some smart tyers maintain a supply though friendly relationships with duck hunters or poulterers. Most tyers, however, will buy their CDC feathers from commercial sources. In Europe, well-known houses like Devaux, from Champagnole in France; Marc Petitjean, from Fribourg in Switzerland and Giorgio Benecchi, from Modena in Italy, are well-known for the quality of their CDC. In the UK, CDC can be obtained from stockists of Veniard's materials and many mail order flytying suppliers list it in their catalogues.

CDC tying - an elegant and simple solution

In 1980, Marjan Fratnik came up with a completely different way of using CDC feathers. His simple and extremely effective patterns marked a new era in the development of CDC flies, some 50 years after the material had first been used.

Marjan Fratnik was born in 1919, in the Slovenian village of Most na Soci (Bridge on the Soca). He learned flyfishing from his father and by watching other experienced fly-fishermen. He caught his first trout on a fly on June 16th 1935 and started a life-long fascination with the pursuit of trout and grayling with the fly rod. In the 1930s, fly fishers in Slovenia used simple traditional English flies. They were all fished in the same manner, since nobody realised there was a difference between wet and dry flies.

Fratnik worked in several countries and travelled all over the world on business. He retired at the age of 68 as an executive of an international company, based in Milan. His cosmopolitan life enabled him to fish all over the world, but he always returned to his beloved home waters in Slovenia. Even now, in his eighties, he still fishes around fifty days every year.

Pausing to retie his fly, Marjan Fratnik on the River Soca.

Marjan Fratnik is a very knowledgeable fly fisher and over the years has devised some very good flies. He is the oldest member of the world famous Ribiska Druzina Tolmin (Tolmin Fishing Club) and is actively involved in the study and protection of the Marble trout of the Soca River basin. From time-to-time he writes on flyfishing for magazines in Slovenia, Italy and Germany and he contributed a chapter on flyfishing history to the Slovenian Flyfishing Manual.

Two of the great masters of CDC, Fratnik and Petitjean, discuss the merits of their flies, midstream. *Didier Martinet.*

Fratnikova puhovka - the F Fly

The F Fly was one of the most effective flies devised in the 1980s and was responsible for many fishermen discovering CDC. In 1977, Fratnik bought a copy of Rindlisbacher's book *Der praktische Fliegenfischer*, from which his interest in CDC was aroused. On his first business trip to Switzerland, Fratnik visited Rindlisbacher's shop and bought some 'Entenbürzelfliegen', in different colours. They were expensive, but they turned out to be extremely good fish catchers. However, after a couple of takes they were beaten up and rendered useless. Fratnik decided to address this problem of vulnerability and, after some experimentation, came up with his own Fratnik Fly. The new fly had all the characteristics he was after. It was easy to tie; it was durable and lasted well; it was visible and easy to see and - last but not least - it proved extremely effective.

The new pattern exceeded his wildest expectations and proved effective on even the most selective trout and grayling. In June 1980, Fratnik gave some F Flies to his friend, Dr. Bozidar Voljc, and it was he who first published an article on the 'Fratnikova puhovka' in 1983 in the Slovenian magazine *Ribic* (The Fisherman). One year later, Fratnik himself published an extensive article on the F Fly in the German magazine *Der Fliegenfischer.*

Since then, the F Fly has gained widespread acclaim. The pattern is amazingly simple. It is just a hook with a few CDC feathers bound to it with tying thread and cut down to size. The body is tied with fine waxed thread in different colours: light grey, yellow, olive or black. Some versions may have a feather fibre or dubbed body. The main reason for the fly's huge popularity is its astonishing attractiveness to fish. The slender body and blurred wing silhouette; the misty grey colour and the way it sits low in the surface film seem to be very insect-like. The F Fly can be used to imitate successfully a whole range of insects, from small emerging and still-born mayflies, to midges and micro caddis.

Now, hundreds of variations of the F Fly have been tied, with various bodies, ribbings, colours and hook types. None seems to have added any extra advantage over the original pattern. Fratnik sometimes ties yellow and orange F Flies, which are more visible and may provide better representations of yellowish stone flies, for example.

F FLY

Hook:	Mustad 94840, size 12—20
Thread:	8/0
Body:	Tying thread
Wing:	One CDC feather for hook size 18– 20; two CDC feathers for sizes 14–16; three CDC feathers for size 12

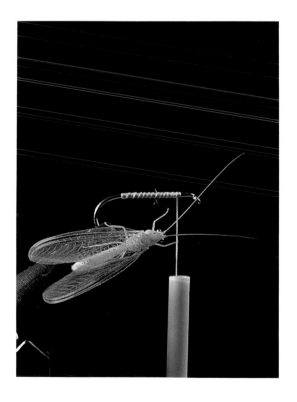

1. As I sat down at the tying vice to construct this F Fly, a lacewing flew in through the window and settled on the hook. Perhaps it too was curious about the Fratnik's fly. In time it departed, and I was able to proceed with the tying (see next page)

2. Take the tying thread down the shank. Fratnik doesn't clip off the loose end, but leaves it long and uses it as a 'ramp' in order to tie a really close-wound thread body. Take the thread back to the eye.

3. Take two or three CDC feathers, depending on quality and hook size. Match them together. Smooth the fibres with thumb and forefinger of the left hand.

4. At this stage, Fratnik clips off waste ends then ties the feathers in on top of the hook, just behind the hook eye. I prefer to tie the feathers in on top of the shank with about five turns of thread, then cut off the waste ends. Push the feather butts away from the hook eye with your thumb nail, and bind them down firmly. Take two turns of thread behind the base of and underneath the feathers to erect them slightly. Make a neat head and whip finish.

5. Trim the CDC feathers to size

F Sedge

In 1985, Fratnik devised this simple impressionistic caddis pattern. The CDC wing is tied in the same style as for the F Fly. The body of the F Sedge consists of thread, with a few wraps of brown cock hackle. Once again, the most important features are silhouette, size and transparency. Fratnik likes no-nonsense patterns. As he puts it: 'A natural fly has only six legs, the body lies on the surface of the water, and there are definitely no gold rings around the body and no red tag.' After years of success in use all over Europe, Fratnik hasn't seen any need to modify the dressing.

When the bats start to flit across the sky, it is time to put on the Netopir

Netopir

Over many years of examining the stomach contents of trout and grayling, Fratnik has come across all sorts of strange incdible objects, including cigarette filter tips, bits of wood and even the end of a yellow pencil! These oddities prompted Fratnik to wonder what the fish actually took them for. Was it some reflex response to a sudden movement, or the vague outline of something that looked edible? In 1990, Fratnik devised his 'monster' fly. It wasn't intended to look like anything particular in the fish's normal diet ...just something that might be good to eat! The Netopir (meaning 'bat') is just a wild bunch of CDC hackles wound on a hook.

Fratnik recommends the Netopir for late afternoon and evening fishing, just after sunset or a little later when bats start to flit. Trout, especially large ones, sometimes leap out of the water to try and grab it. The best time of the year to fish the Netopir is from the middle of May to the end of June. Sometimes, pulling the fly under the water in front of the fish's nose can provoke a take. It can also be extremely effective in very fast water during the daytime, especially for trout in April and for grayling in the second part of May. For big marble trout, Fratnik recommends a Netopir tied on large long shank hooks (size 6—8), which must be weighted and fished on sink tip lines or fast sinking tippets. Large Netopirs are very difficult to keep down on the bottom since they tend to want to pop up to the surface all the time.

New patterns

Lately, Fratnik has experimented with three new patterns:

FF

This CDC palmer is a real Fratnik fly. It doesn't look like anything in particular, but even fussy fish can be fooled by its suggestiveness of a wide range of insects. It could resemble a fluttering egg-laying mayfly, perhaps, or a sedge or a stonefly. The FF is tied with one hackled CDC feather that can be clipped before or after winding. The FF floats high at first, then tends to settle down into the surface film, both of which can be very attractive to fish. Fratnik says that ugly FFs are better fish catchers than perfectly tied examples. He likes a few stray fibres here and there.

F Bug

After observing larvae falling from the bushes and taken by trout, Fratnik created the F Bug (*pictured below*). It's a 'monstrosity' that should be used in the evening, slightly sunk in the film for fussy grayling in slow moving riffles. Usually tied in size 12—14, the yellow version is a little more visible, but both yellow and grey catch fish equally well. The body is of CDC dubbing; the back is made of a CDC feather.

When you anticipate catching a big trout, the F Streamer, probably a fry imitation, is the one to use.

F Streamer

In the wonderful Soca River lives the marble trout *(Salmo trutta marmoratus)*. This unique and endangered species is much sought-after by anglers. The main reason for its decline is its interbreeding with brown trout that were introduced into the area just before the end of the 19th century. The upper reaches of the Soca and its tributaries are rocky and have fast currents that hold good stocks of genetically pure marble trout.

Woolly Buggers have proved very effective lures for marble trout and inspired Fratnik to devise his own CDC streamer on which he has caught marble trout up to 55cm. He is very enthusiastic about this pattern and reckons it would be a good salmon fly as well. He fishes it like any other streamer, with fast pulls and a bend of the wrist at the end of each stroke to give the fly a short vertical jerk. He uses the F Streamer wherever he expects to encounter a big fish, or where trout haven't responded to a dry fly or nymph. Fish normally take at the end of the pull, when the streamer stops moving.

Marjan Fratnik has been a well known personality in the flyfishing world for a long time. Over the years he has devised some fine patterns, not only CDC. His name will, however, always be associated with his F Fly and F Sedge. I'm sure they will be around long after many other patterns have been forgotten.

and the CDC hackle

Gerhard Laible is an innovative German flytyer who has done a great deal of work with CDC since the mid-1980s. Through his lectures and demonstrations and the publication of a book and numerous articles on the subject, Laible has been largely responsible for the popularity of CDC flies in the German speaking countries.

Above: Gerhard Laible, a master at the vice when it comes to CDC tying.
Left: Marc Petitjean fishing the Soca river. *Photos by Rudy van Duijnhoven*

Gerhard Laible was born in 1952 in Malsch, near Karlsruhe. He still lives there and works in telecommunications. Although an angler since childhood, he first started flyfishing in 1980 and took up flytying at about the same time. These days he likes to fish the rivers of Slovenia, the Frankische Schweitz in Germany, and the French Jura.

Early on in his flytying career, Laible came across a traditional Swiss-style CDC fly, obtained from a German firm. He was puzzled by its beautiful CDC hackle. Carefully dissecting the fly, he discovered that the hackle was nothing but a normally wound CDC

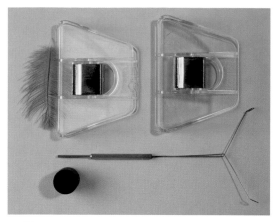

Laible's CDC spinning set: two paper clamps, and a small weight to add to the twister to make for faster spinning.

feather. From then on, Laible started experimenting to achieve his own perfect Moustique. After some time he succeeded, not by winding the feather, but by mounting separate bunches of fibres around the hook shank. This novel method was rather complicated and time consuming. Nevertheless, Laible's early trials were important for they opened up a new approach to possibilities with CDC. They paved the way for later developments that were explored both by Laible himself, and by Marc Petitjean.

Flies and publications

Die Danica-Sequenz

In 1986 Laible published an article 'In meiner Technik: Die Danica - Sequenz' *(Der Fliegenfischer* 65) on patterns to represent the emerger, dun and spent spinner stages of *Ephemera danica*. In this article he presented some novel uses of CDC. For the dun and spinner, he used CDC feathers for the wings. In the emerger, he used CDC over the thorax to form the wing case. One particularly noteworthy application was Laible's use of CDC for dubbing. He mixed seal's fur and CDC fibres for the bodies.

Pfandlen or PK method

In the same year, 1986, another distinguished German tyer, Robert Pfandl, also published a series of articles in *Der Fliegenfischer*. Pfandl introduced the method of mixing various materials like feather fibres and hair with the help of a mixing bloc, paper clamps and a dubbing twister. This ingenious technique opened up many possibilities and in Germany became known as 'Pfandlen' (pfandling). The second article in Pfandl's series was especially significant because it showed CDC fibres being put into a dubbing loop to create an attractive, rugged, CDC hackle.

For the record, however, Robert Pfandl did not originate this use of paper clamps in flytying. That honour goes to Hans Kievits, a fellow member of my own fly-fishing club in Vlaardingen, Holland. I first saw Hans working with large metal paper clamps and loops of fine copper wire to twist strands of fur and deer hair long before 1986. Hans named this technique the 'PK method' after the Dutch word 'papierklem' (paper clamp). Hans told me that he had demonstrated the PK method to Germans in the Pension Eisenberger, on the Weiße Traun, in 1985. After this trip to Southern Germany, Hans' method must have somehow found its way to Robert Pfandl.

Vom Cul de Canard

Using the PK/Pfandlen method, Gerhard Laible developed the majority of his CDC flies, which he presented in his 'Vom Cul de Canard' series of articles, again in *Der Fliegenfischer*. The first of these articles appeared in 1988 and the series is still running some 13 years later. Each article describes a number of patterns, with step-by-step tying instructions. While Laible provides at best only brief explanations on how these patterns should be fished, his articles have never the less had quite an impact in Germany and bordering countries, including Holland.

In the earliest of his articles, Pfandl showed a remarkable innovation where CDC and peacock herl are spun together in a dubbing loop and used for the bodies of the Bürzel Caddis (CDC Caddis) and Bürzel Palmer (CDC Palmer). This style set the trend for many more of Liable's CDC patterns that have appeared since then.

BÜRZELPALMER

Hook:	TMC 5230, size 10—16
Thread:	Uni thread 8/0 black
Body:	Peacock herl
Hackle:	Two medium size CDC feathers

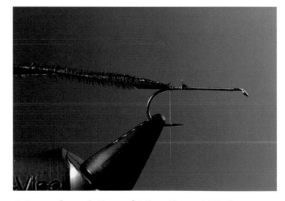

1. Lay a foundation of tying thread. Tie in two peacock herls just in front of the hook bend.

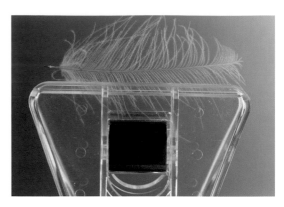

2. Form a dubbing loop, exactly at the point where the herls are mounted. The loop should be a little longer than the herls. Close the loop carefully with an extra turn of thread against the shank. Lightly wax the thread loop.

3. Place two CDC feathers onto each other, concave to concave and tip to butt. Clamp the fibres of one side of both feathers in a paper clamp and clip them off with a long pair of scissors as close to the stem as possible. Repeat this procedure with a second clamp.

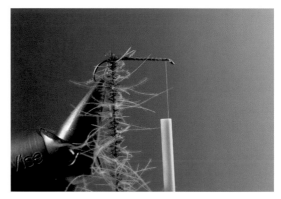

4. Open the loop and insert the fibres. Spread the fibres evenly over a length slightly less than that of the herls. Grasp the loop and the herls with a pair of hackle pliers and spin together to produce a 'rope' of peacock herl and CDC.

5. Wind this rope around the shank with the right hand (assuming a right-hander). Use your left hand to groom the fibres out of the way so that none get trapped under subsequent wraps.

6. If you wish to form a sort of thorax, you can over wind in this area, but keep controlling the fibres by pulling them out of the way with the left hand. Tie off the rope with a few turns of tying thread and snip away the waste.

7. Form a neat head with the tying thread, whip finish and clip the CDC fibres to desired length.

Using the loop method, Laible produces robust, but fairly bulky patterns. Moreover, his combination of CDC with various other materials - peacock herl, deer hair, moufflon hair and various synthetics - reinforces this effect. It is a feature recurrent in his articles. However, while Laible's patterns have a robustness and bulk that is sometimes desirable, it is at the expense of the delicate character that characterised the early Swiss and French CDC patterns and those developed later on by Marjan Fratnik.

What, one may ask, is the point of mixing CDC with stiffer and much 'heavier' materials? In his very first article 'Die kombinierte Elementbehechelung' *(Der Fliegenfischer* 61,1985), Laible explained his reason for combining CDC and a cock hackle. On the one hand, he liked the action and transparency of CDC, and on the other, he liked the spring and gleam of cock hackles. It seemed logical to him to try and take advantage of the best features of both materials. In developing this, Laible experimented with many existing patterns: replacing certain element of the original dressing with CDC (e.g. Laible's CDC version of the Red Tag).

In my opinion, one of Laible's most interesting articles is Vom Cul de Canards number V *(Der Fliegenfischer* 87,1990), devoted to making flies with CDC parachute hackles. In my experience, parachute hackles are an extremely effective use of CDC. The emerger and dun pattern Laible describes in that article float flat in the film. The soft silhouette and the action of the wet fibres in the surface are particularly appealing.

PARA-EMERGER

Hook:	TMC 5230, size 12—18
Thread:	Uni thread 8/0 black
Tail:	Brown cock hackle fibres
Body:	Brown mink dubbing
Wing case:	Polycelon (colours yellow, black, white, etc.)
Hackle:	CDC fibres

1. Attach thread and wind to a position directly above the hook point. Secure a bunch of cock hackle fibres on top of the hook. Push the tails slightly erect by taking a turn of thread under the cock fibres.

2. Take the strip of Polycelon and tie it in one quarter of the hook shank from the eye.

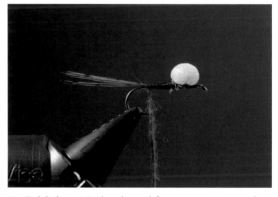

3. Fold the strip back and form a neat round wing case. Tie off and snip away the excess.

4. Take the thread back to the tails; spin the mink dubbing onto the thread and wind an abdomen close up to the polypropylene wing case.

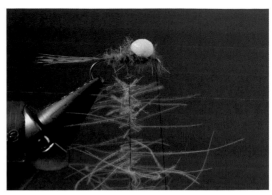

5. Take two CDC feathers and smooth the fibres back (from tip to but). Put the feathers with concave sides together; butt on tip, tip on butt. Clasp the fibres of one side with a paper clamp and clip off close to the stem. Repeat this procedure on the other side of the feathers.

6. Make a loop with the tying thread at the base of the wing case two times the length of one CDC feather. Close the loop by taking one firm turn of thread around the base of the loop. Apply a pinch of dubbing to the thread and form the thorax (under the Polycelon wing pad). Lightly wax the thread loop and insert the CDC fibres into the loop. Twist the loop to form a fine CDC 'hackle'.

7. Wrap the twisted loop around the base of the wing case, carefully grooming the fibres with the other hand, so as to trap as few fibres as possible under the succeeding turns. Stop as soon as a nice parachute hackle has formed. Tie off the loop with the tying thread, and snip off the excess. Add some more dubbing to the thread and wind on to form a head to the fly, before whip finishing just behind the hook eye. Finally, trim the CDC parachute fibres to the desired length with sharp scissors.

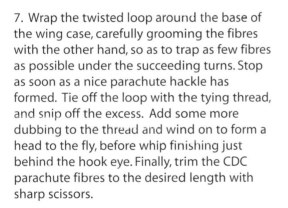

In the 1990s, Laible became better known outside Germany and in 1991 he switched to using the increasingly ubiquitous term 'CDC' (Vom Cul de Canard VIII article (*Der Fliegenfischer* 98,1991). His Bürzel Caddis and Bürzel Palmer patterns had their names changed to CDC Caddis and CDC Palmer. Eventually, the famous American company, Umpqua Feather Merchants, started selling some of his patterns. These are also available in Germany from Traun River Products, which also sells the special tools developed by Laible for his CDC loop method.

Emerger and dun from Gerhard Laible's Danica-Sequenz

The first book on CDC

In 1993, Laible published *CDC Flies* - the first book devoted exclusively to CDC. It gives information on CDC and fishing with CDC patterns. The book also discusses natural insects and the author's own patterns, most of which have appeared in his articles. While the book and articles complement each other well, it is a bit of a pity that both are needed to get the complete picture.

Over many years, Gerhard Laible has made a valuable contribution to the technical development of tying with CDC feathers and inspired many by his writings on the subject. He can justifiably be considered the instigator of the German 'CDC school'. In his footsteps have followed such well-known tyers as Henning von Monteton, Gerd-Peter Wieditz and Andreas Hecht, who have gone on to develop their own ways with CDC.

New ideas and new patterns for CDC

Probably more than anyone else, Marc Petitjean has been responsible for the huge popularity that CDC flies have today. He has developed a considerable collection of CDC fly patterns and made commercially available the feathers and tools needed to tie them. His products are distinguished by their quality and the originality of thought that Marc has brought to flytying.

Marc Petitjean was born in 1955 in Troyes, France. At fourteen, he started experimenting with his grandfather's split cane rod and an old line that needed frequent greasing to stay afloat. In 1978, Marc went to work in Fribourg, Switzerland. With the region's numerous fine rivers, it was here that flyfishing really took hold of him, learning from anglers of the calibre of Louis Limouzin and Michel Roggo. During this time, he became interested in CDC flies, inspired by Gerhard Laible's unorthodox tying techniques published in *Der Fliegenfischer*. But it was not until 1986 that Marc started working seriously on his own CDC designs.

By the late 1980s, Marc had devised a complete series of CDC flies and was considering turning professional as a flytyer. He had made the acquaintance of Louis Veya, an elderly Swiss professional tyer, who quickly recognised that there was something special about Petitjean's flies. Veya helped Marc in every possible way, even supplying him with a considerable quantity of CDC feathers.

In April 1990, Marc gave his first presentation at a show at Hilden, near Düsseldorf, organised by *Der Fliegenfischer* magazine. In May of the same year, he attended the Fly Fair, in the Netherlands. On both occasions he encountered tremendous enthusiasm for his flies and techniques.

Over the years, tyers have tried to copy his patterns with more or (usually) less success. His technique of tying split-wing duns, for instance, has been particularly puzzling.

Marc Petitjean duns, some with split wings.

By 'anatomising', people could detect the tying process, but not the details. While tying a fly for me during an interview, he pointed at the wings of a nearly finished dun. With a smile he said: 'Some people are pretty frustrated, because they don't know what these wings look like before they are cut. They can only see what is left!' He went on tying and explained that it wasn't just a matter of understanding but, more importantly, of practice. Even after fully understanding the processes involved, it would take most tyers several dozen attempts before they could turn out a proper MP. To demonstrate his point, Marc showed me how to pick fibres from a CDC feather, then told me to try and do the same. It proved much harder than it had looked when he did it and I ended up ruining a precious CDC feather.

MPs don't just look pretty, they are imitative and effective. In *The Complete Fly-fisher's Handbook* (1998), Malcolm Greenhalgh wrote: ' If you can only afford a few, it is worth keeping them for particularly selective or difficult trout or grayling that have refused more conventional flies. An appropriate CDC pattern will often take these fastidious fish.'

Series 1

Marc's first series of flies, from 1989, can be considered the basis of the MP collection. The most striking feature is that all sixteen flies are composed almost entirely of CDC. Whole CDC feathers are used for the bodies, while the wings are made of bunches of CDC fibres. Only the tails of some of the flies are tied with cock hackle fibres. All of these flies look quite simple: superfluous elements are left out.

MPs are devised to imitate natural insects and there is an MP design for almost any hatch one is likely to encounter. Marc Petitjean is adamant on one point: '...the most important features of a dry fly are size and silhouette. Colour is more important to the fisherman than to the fish, since, most of the time, the fish sees the fly in silhouette against the light.'

MP's bodies rest on the surface film, while the hook bend is under the surface. This gives them good balance and tends to keep them sitting upright. Moreover, it confers better hooking than with high riding, traditionally hackled flies, especially with grayling. MP's are also better imitations than traditional flies because emerging insects spend more time in the water film, rather than riding high on the surface.

Opposite: Marc Petitjean brings in a fine marmorata trout on the River Koritnica, Slovenia.

Split winged duns (MP 10, 11, 13, 14, 16, 19, 21 and 22)

There has been some discussion about the imitative correctness of Marc's split wing duns. Many people believe that an ephemerid fly either has its wings upright and closed together (dun stage), or spread out on the water (spent stage). Few realise that, immediately after emergence from the nymph, ephemerids hold their wings slightly apart in order for them to dry and harden off properly. It is at this vulnerable stage that the insects are particularly attractive to the fish. MP's split wing duns were designed to imitate this stage.

Caddis (MP 52 and 53)

MP's Series 1 also contains some caddis (sedge) patterns. MP 52 matches the many dark caddis species, such as occur frequently in Scandinavia. These are very effective for evening and night fishing. MP 53 imitates the lighter species, such as the Brown Sedge and Caperer.

MP 52 (CADDIS)

Hook:	TMC 5230, size 12–16
Thread:	Black 8/0
Body:	Long CDC feather (MP 6)
Wing:	CDC fibres (MP 6)

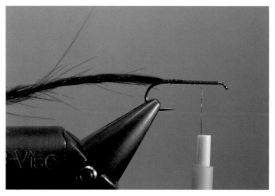

1. Run the tying thread down the hook shank to the start of the bend. Prepare the CDC feather to be used for the body by twisting it in one direction. Tie in the twisted feather by the tip, at the start of the hook bend and run the thread back up the shank to a point one quarter of the shank length behind the eye.

2. Wind the CDC feather three quarters of the way up the hook shank, towards the eye. Maintain the twist in the feather, after each turn. Tie down the feather at this point, with firm turns of thread. Do NOT cut away the remaining butt end of the CDC feather, which is still required.

3. Pick a bunch of fibres from a CDC feather and tie them in for the wing. Run the thread up to just behind the hook eye.

4. Now, take about two more turns of the CDC body feather, in front of the wing. Tie in at the head with at least four firm turns of thread. Snip away the waste end of the feather.

5. Wind a head, whip finish and trim the wing to desired length.

Petit Merdes (MP 63, 64, 65 and 66)

These MPs are tied like the caddis flies, but they are smaller and can be considered as general patterns. They are tied in different colours to represent all of those little beasts that are so hard to identify on occasions: e.g. micro caddis, smuts, black gnats, etc.

Special Patterns (MP 71 and 72)

MP 71 imitates an ant, hawthorn fly, or even a black beetle. MP 72 has a yellow body with black rings and can be used to suggest wasps, bees, hover flies, etc.

Marc Petijean's midge patterns, left column, adult midges (MP 67, 68), centre column emergent pupae (MP 48, 47), right column midge larvae (MP 37, 39).

Series 2

In 1992, Petitjean devised a second series of flies, with some interesting innovations. He astonished the fly-fishing world by his introduction of subsurface CDC patterns! Before this happened, CDC had been used only for tying floating flies.

Weighted Nymphs
(MP 31, 32, 33, 34 and 76)

Since nymphs are presented in the same element as the fish, the quarry can scrutinise them far more closely. For nymphs, therefore, colour, shape and anatomical details need to be more accurately rendered than in a dry fly. MP's nymph tails contain bunches of speckled Coq de León fibres on either side of the hook. The abdomen is conical, while mobile CDC fibres are used to imitate the legs.

Stone Flies, Marc Petijean from top left, 89, 87, 36.

Freshwater Shrimps (MP 76)

This notable subsurface pattern represents a freshwater shrimp (scud) in its breeding coloration. Short CDC fibres imitate the crustacean's multiple legs.

Emergers
(MP 41, 42, 43 and 44)

In his second series, Marc devised these representations addressed specifically at emerging ephemerids. On occasions, fish become preoccupied with this stage of the insect's development as they struggle helplessly in the surface film. In these patterns, wing cases are formed by folding forward a bunch of CDC, which traps air very effectively. This provides buoyancy for the front of the fly, while the hook bend and rear part of the body sinks below the surface. The hook bend is weighted with silver wire, which also gives it an attractive extra sparkle. There are four colour variations.

Petitjean's Shrimps & Bugs, top to bottom, Dragonfly nymph, Damselfly nymph, Freshwater shrimp.(breeding colours)

This is a selection of Marc Petitjean caddis patterns. Clockwise, from top left: MP 91 (larva), MP 74 (emerger pupa, MP 56 (adult), MP 65 & 63 (la petite merde), MP 52 (adult).

MP 43 (EMERGER)

Hook:	TMC 100, size 12—16
Thread:	8/0 black
Tail:	Coq de León feather fibres, Brown Uni Stretch floss
Abdomen:	Olive CDC feather (MP 8)
Ribbing:	Silver wire
Wing case:	Olive CDC fibres (MP 8)
Thorax:	Same feather as for abdomen

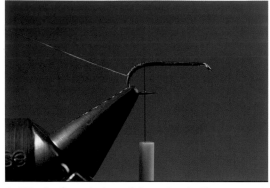

1. Wind a foundation of thread to halfway round the hook bend. Tie in a length of silver wire, then take the thread to the end of the shank.

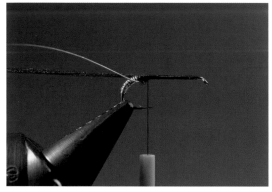

2. Make touching turns of wire up to the rear end of the shank. Then, tie in a doubled length of Uni Stretch at the end of the shank.

3. Tie in Coq de León fibres on top of the hook shank, then and pull the Uni Stretch up between the tail fibres to split the bunch into two equal halves.

4. Secure the Uni Stretch and clip off the excess.

5. Prepare the CDC feather by twisting it in one direction. Tie it in by the tip.

6. Wind the abdomen while twisting the feather; less twisting at the end sector of the abdomen. Tie it down firmly. Do not cut away the excess feather. Rib the abdomen with silver wire.

7. Pick fibres from a CDC feather and tie in.

8. Wind the thorax, continuing with the abdomen feather, maintaining the twist. Secure the CDC and trim off the waste.

9. Fold the wing case fibres over the thorax to forming a rounded hump. Trap the fibres with a few turns of thread, before folding back the fibre ends and binding them down with the thread.

10. Wind a head and whip finish.

Caddis Pupa (MP 74)

This Caddis pupa imitation looks most convincing with its ribbed but shaggy body, its opening wing buds (represented by two feathers folded forward) and CDC fibres sticking out to suggest the legs.

Spent Spinner (MP 81, 82)

This pattern is a spent fly, coming in two colours: red and dark brown.

Further Series

After 1992, Marc extended his fly collection in stages. He devised more leaded subsurface flies, including Caddis Larvae (MP 91 and 92); Heptagenid nymphs (MP 95 and 96); a darker *Gammarus* imitation (MP 77) and high floating nymphs (MP 25 and 27).

Some important omissions from his earlier series were now introduced, including: an *Ephemera danica* emerger (MP 45); an adult *E. danica* (MP 14/10); mayflies in the adult stage with closed wings (MP 12 and 15); the *E. danica* spent-spinner (MP 85) and a large and very light adult caddis (MP 54).

Clockwise, from top left: MPs 31, 33, 96, 27 (all nymphs), 44, 43, 41 (all emergers)

Series 4, 5 and 6 are at least as remarkable as the nymph series since they contain streamers for salmon and sea trout (MP 210, 212 and 214); for steelhead (216, 218 and 220); for bonefish (MP 650, 652, 654 and 656 - all unweighted; MP 660, 662, 664, 666 - all weighted). There is even a modular streamer that can be adjusted for length and colour for predatory fish, such as pike and the various bass species (MP 310, 312 and 314 - all sinkable and 350, 352 and 354 - all floating).

MP 220 (STEELHEAD STREAMER)

Hook:	TMC 9444, size 4–6
Thread:	8/0 black
Body:	Copper wire, white and green fluo. floss
Hackle:	Long light yellow (MP 10) and fluo. red (MP 9) CDC feather

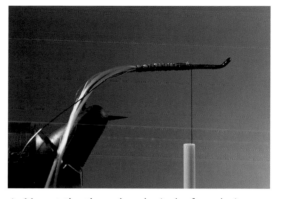

1. Mount the thread and wind a foundation down the hook shank. Tie in the copper wire, the white and green floss.

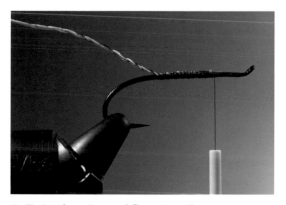

2. Twist the wire and floss together.

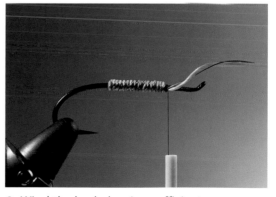

3. Wind the body, leaving sufficient space behind the hook eye for the hackle.

4. Smooth back the fibres of one yellow and one red CDC feather. Place together, with the yellow feather underneath, then tie them both in by the tips, with the dull undersides facing backwards. Clip off the waste tips.

5. Carefully wind the feathers together, in close turns, towards the hook eye. Smooth back the fibres as you wind, being careful not to trap any fibres as you go. Stop winding when the feather stems become too thick. Tie down with firm turns of thread and snip off the waste butts of the feathers.

6. Wind a neat head and whip finish.

In recent years Marc Petitjean has gone on to devise many more patterns, imitating midges, stoneflies, beetles, ants, grasshoppers, water boatmen, tadpoles and other creatures. His entire collection is now quite extensive. It has been necessary for me to try and make a representative selection of what I consider to be his most generally useful dry flies, emergers, nymphs and streamers. Inevitably, I have had to leave out many patterns from this remarkable innovator. It is due largely to Marc Petitjean that CDC flies have become so widely known and generally popular throughout the fly-fishing world.

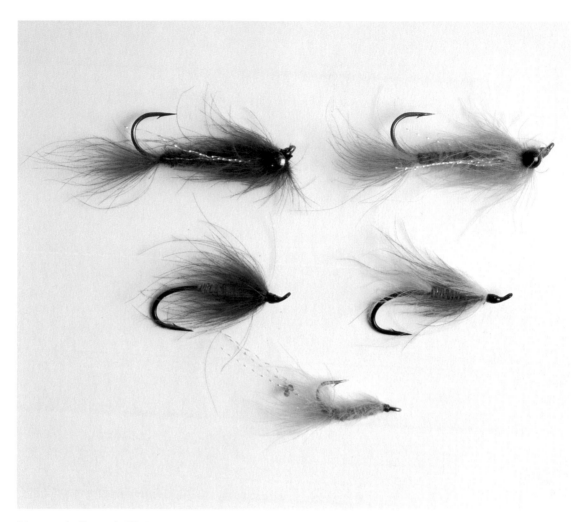

Marc was the first to tie CDC streamers: here are five of them: (clockwise, top left) MPs 110, 112, 210, 664, 218

Marc Petitjean's work with CDC had a major influence on flyfishing in the 1990s. In his wake, other flytyers have incorporated this extraordinary and versatile material into their own patterns, pushing back the frontiers of development with CDC with new ideas.

In this chapter, I have assembled an international group of outstanding flytyers and their CDC patterns. All of them are convinced of the remarkable virtues of CDC and use it, either for essential elements in certain patterns, or as the complete material from which the whole fly is tied. Some of my own flies are included here as well.

Tying with CDC has undergone revolutionary development since the original Swiss Moustique patterns. The space of little more than a decade has seen its increasing use in all kinds of patterns and fishing styles. During the last few years, a new trend has emerged. From the start, the value of CDC in dry flies was recognised and this will probably always be its principal role. Lately, however, its use 'in the film' and in sub-surface patterns has grown considerably. These developments are still in their early stages and it's likely that even the exiting new ground will be broken as inventive flytyers continue to explore the properties of this unique material.

Theo Bakelaar

Each year, Theo Bakelaar visits Scotland for several weeks, where he guides anglers to the lovely hills in pursuit of wild brown trout; to the rivers for salmon and sea trout and to the coast after mackerel and other salt water species. This annual pilgrimage and its varied fishing has afforded Theo many opportunities to experiment with CDC flies.

Theo Bakelaar with a superb Lake Oostvoorne rainbow

Here he recalls the effectiveness of one particular pattern.

"As I sit in my tying room, with the haunting strains of a Scottish ballad on the hi-fi in the background, my imagination is transported to that lovely country of mountains, lochs and rivers. My memories turn to fishing a small spate stream, up in the hills, yet not far from the sea. Here there is a chance of sea trout and maybe, even a salmon. As the incessant wind subsides for a moment I tie on my flies. On the top dropper, I put on a little blue CDC sea trout fly with silver body, tied on a small double. It is one of my best flies: my own variation of existing patterns like the Silver Doctor. The tail fly will be a CDC Green Highlander. My guess is there will be salmon around.

Until recently, salmon and sea trout flies were rarely tied with CDC fibres, yet this material lends itself to the sparse, ethereal styles that can be so effective for sea trout - especially during the daytime. CDC fibres are mobile and translucent and trap air bubbles under water. It's the combination of these qualities and the way the CDC releases its little stream of bubbles underwater that I'm sure contribute to its attraction. In my mind's eye I can recall the swing of the flies, then the sudden electric snatch of the take as the line is jerked violently out of my hand.

After the unforgettable wildness of the fight, a beautiful fresh silver sea trout comes to hand. Yet again, it's that little blue and silver dropper fly that has done the damage: slim, sparse, agile, air bubbles—deadly!"

1. CDC BLUE AND SILVER

Hook: Partridge double, size 8—14

Thread: Danville black 8/0

Body: Flat silver tinsel

Rib: Thin round silver tinsel

Legs/hackle: One hackled CDC feather dyed blue, black CDC fibres tied in over the hackle

2. BLACK AND RED CDC

Hook: Partridge double, size 8—14

Thread: Danville black 8/0

Body: Black CDC dubbing

Rib: Fine gold thread

Legs/hackle: One hackled CDC feather dyed black, with red CDC fibres tied in over the hackle

Top row: CDC Blue & Silver, Theo's No-Name Salmon Fly, Black & Red CDC
Second row: CDC Jungle Cock variant, Blue Zulu CDC, CDC Willie Gunn Double
Third row: CDC Green Highlander variant, CDC Seatrout Fly
Bottom row: CDC Shrimp Double (red & rose variants)

3. THEO'S NO NAME SALMON

Hook:	Partridge double, size 8—14
Thread:	Danville black 8/0
Tail:	Black CDC fibres
Body:	CDC dubbing yellow, hackled black CDC feather, green glittering strip
Legs/hackle:	One hackled CDC feather dyed yellow, one hackled black CDC feather

4. BLUE ZULU CDC

Hook:	TMC 760 TC, any size
Thread:	Danville black 8/0
Tail:	Red CDC fibres
Body:	Black CDC dubbing
Legs/hackle:	One hackled CDC feather dyed blue

5. CDC WILLIE GUNN DOUBLE

Hook:	Partridge double, any size
Thread:	Danville black 8/0
Body:	Black floss
Ribbing:	Thin gold thread
Legs/hackle:	One hackled CDC feather dyed yellow, one hackled CDC feather dyed orange, one hackled black CDC feather

6. CDC GREEN HIGHLANDER VARIANT

Hook:	Partridge double, any size
Thread:	Danville black 8/0
Tail:	Yellow CDC fibres
Body:	Green glitter strip
Legs/hackle:	Hackled CDC feathers dyed green

7. CDC SEA TROUT FLY

Hook:	Partridge double, size 8—14
Thread:	Danville black 8/0
Tail:	Red hackled CDC feather or red CDC fibres
Body:	Flat silver tinsel
Legs/hackle:	Hackled CDC feathers dyed blue

8. CDC JUNGLE COCK VARIATION

Hook:	Partridge double, size 8—14
Thread:	Danville black 8/0
Tail:	Orange/yellow CDC fibres
Body:	Black floss
Ribbing:	Thin round gold tinsel
Legs/hackle:	Hackled black CDC feathers
Eyes:	Jungle cock

9. CDC SHRIMP DOUBLE (RED AND ROSE)

Hook:	Partridge double, size 8—14
Thread:	Danville or nylon matching the colour
Eyes:	melted nylon
Antennae:	Halo glitter and CDC fibres same colour
Body:	Hackled CDC feather same colour
Tail:	Hackled CDC feather or CDC fibres
Legs/hackle:	CDC feathers cut into shape

Hans van Klinken

My friends Hans and Ina van Klinken are the most dedicated of flyfishers. They have fished extensively in Scandinavia, the UK and in Canada. Hans is one of the most inventive flytyers I know. Among his best-known creations are the Klinkhåmer Special, Leadhead and Caseless Caddis. He has also designed several successful Atlantic salmon flies and these CDC patterns.

Hans van Klinken with a 50cm grayling caught with the Culard on the River Glomma, Norway.

1. RUGGED CADDIS

The first breakthrough Hans made with CDC was this one, derived from the Swedish sedge pattern called the Rackelhanen. The natural colour of the CDC feathers was perfect to imitate dark grey sedges. Hans uses the Rugged Caddis mainly for Atlantic salmon and Arctic char in northern Norway. The Jagged Caddis is a bigger variation, tied with a hackle, on small streamer hooks.

Hook: Partridge L3A, size 6—8
Thread: Uni-thread 8/0 black
Body: Rabbit or squirrel dubbing, dyed dark grey
Wing: Sixteen CDC feathers, tied in four sections

2. CULARD SEDGE

The Culard Sedge is another realistic pattern devised to imitate a smaller dark grey sedge.

Hook: Partridge E1A, size 12—14
Thread: Uni-thread 8/0 black
Rib: Extra fine gold wire
Body: Herl fibres from a black peacock wing feather
Hackle: Dark blue dun
Wing: Four CDC feathers
Wing case: CDC feathers (same as wing)
Thorax: Rabbit or squirrel dubbing dyed dark grey
Antennae: Two black bear fibres (substitute paintbrush fibres)

3. CULARD

Not to be confused with the Culard Sedge, this excellent fly was devised as an emerger pattern for low water conditions on rivers from Central Europe up to the Scandinavian north. Fishing the Culard subsurface is especially deadly on still waters, when fish are feeding just under the surface. Hans used to moisten this pattern to drown it and fish it as a subsurface emerger, until he devised the soft hackle Culard. He believes it is the halo effect produced by the air bubble trapped by the wing that is responsible for this pattern's effectiveness.

Hook: Partridge E1A size 18, or E6A, size 16—18

Thread: Uni-thread 8/0 black

Body: Herl fibres from the black wing feather of a peacock

Rib: Extra fine gold wire or yellow Pearsall's silk

Wing: Four CDC feathers cut half way the body

Hackle: Four turns of fine dark blue dun cock hackle.

N.B. For Culards intended to be fished subsurface, hackle with starling body feather

These are Hans Van Klinken's flies: Clockwise from top left Rugged Caddis, Culard, Jagged Caddis, Culard Dun, Once and Away Emerger, and Culara Dun.

4. CULARD DUN

There are two versions of the Culard Dun. The first is not very well known but well worth trying. The second version is tied parachute style. Both are very effective river patterns.

DRESSING 1

Hook:	Partridge E1A, size 12—22
Thread:	Uni-thread 8/0 grey
Tail:	CDC
Body:	CDC and thread
Wing:	CDC tied up vertically

DRESSING 2

Hook:	Partridge E1A, size 12—18
Thread:	Uni-thread 8/0 grey
Butt:	Fly-Rite golden brown No.17 dubbing (BCS 66/62) dubbed very sparsely
Tail:	Four Microfibetts dyed dark dun, split in two sections
Rib:	Pearsall's No. 6a
Body:	Fly-Rite dark olive brown No. 42 dubbing (BCS 34)
Hackle:	Dark dun tied in parachute style
Wing:	CDC

5. CULARA DUN

This is Hans' CDC adaptation of an existing Scandinavian pattern, tied in Comparadun style. Unfortunately, Hans doesn't know the author of the original pattern. Hans ties variations with olive, dun and grey body colours.

Hook:	Partridge E1A, size 12—14
Thread:	Uni-thread 8/0
Butt:	Fly-Rite dubbing tied very sparsely
Tail:	Four Microfibetts tied in two sections
Rib:	Fine tinsel or Pearsall's silk
Body:	Fly-Rite dubbing (colour after personal preference)
Wing:	Four CDC feathers tied forward (pretty long)
Legs:	Hackle wound as collar behind the wing and cut at bottom

6. ONCE AND AWAY EMERGER

The Once and Away Emerger is a very effective pattern at the start of a hatch when flies begin to emerge. Hans is convinced that it is the silhouette of the fly that induces the take. This fly works well in lakes as well as on rivers and is Hans' first choice when he can't decide what else to put on.

Hook:	Partridge GRS 12ST, size 12—16
Thread:	Uni-thread 8/0
Tail:	Four Microfibetts split in two sections
Tag:	Green or orange tying silk
Rib:	Extra fine tinsel or Pearsall's silk
Body:	CDC or Fly-Rite dubbing (colour after personal preference)
Wing:	Four CDC feathers natural or dyed olive
Thorax:	CDC (natural or olive)
Wing case:	CDC feathers

7. CULARD PARACHUTE EMERGER

This is a larger CDC pattern that Hans devised some years after his Klinkhåmer. The fly is popular among Hans' Finnish friends for tempting those large grayling in the north. The original fly was tied in an olive colour, but subsequently, a black variation has turned out to be more successful.

Hook:	Partridge D3ST or 12ST, size 12—8
Thread:	Uni-thread 8/0 black or grey
Rib:	Yellow Pearsall's silk
Body:	Herl fibres of a black peacock wing feather

Hackle: Blue, light or dark dun tied in parachute-style
Wing 1:   Four CDC feathers
Thorax: Peacock herl
Wing 2:   Four CDC feathers
Wing case: CDC (same as wing 2 and tied down after the parachute is finished)

8. ONCE AND AWAY

An effective emerger pattern for both still water and river fishing. Hans called it the 'Once and Away' since he had a great difficulty in getting his first versions of this fly to float again after they had been drowned by fish. The problem was overcome when Hans started tying the fly with larger feathers, trimmed down to the desired length. By having the larger (stiffer) CDC shafts supporting the wing tuft, Hans found that the fly's floatability could be recovered with a few false casts.

Hook: Partridge GRS 15ST, size 12—18
Thread: Uni-thread 8/0 black
Body: A single peccary fibre, wound to give a ribbed effect
Wing: Four large CDC feathers of whatever colour you prefer. Larger flies may need more plumes
Thorax: Three or four peacock herls
Wing case: CDC feathers (same as wing)

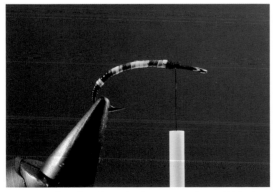

1. Wrap the shank with the tying thread. Tie in the peccary fibre (or any quill as substitute) at the tail and wind in touching turns to form a fine tapered body.

2. Tie in four large CDC feathers together with three peacock herls. You may need as many as six CDC feathers on larger sizes and if using only small feathers.

3. Wind the peacock herls to form the thorax.

4. Pull the CDC feathers over the thorax and tie them down just behind the eye.

5. Bring the feathers into an upright position and secure them with the tying thread, with maybe a tiny drop of varnish at the roots of the wing. Be careful not to ruin the CDC by allowing too much varnish to soak into the fibres. Trim the feathers to size, to suit the imitation, or your preference.

---

9. MIGHTY MIDGE

This is Hans' favourite midge imitation when large fish are feeding on chironomids.

Hook: Partridge K 14ST, size 16—18

Thread: Uni-thread 8/0 black

Tail: One or two fine tips from the smallest blue dun hackle

Wing: Four small CDC feathers

Thorax: Two small strands of peacock herl

Wing case: CDC feathers (same as wing)

Fishing the 'Once and Away' at Hodalen

by Hans van Klinken

"On a high mountain plateau in Norway, between Tolga and Lake Fermund, is a series of interconnected lakes on the river Hola. The Lakes of Hodalen have become one of my favourite locations in Europe for still water grayling fishing. The area is tough and rugged, prone to strong mountain winds and quick changes of weather, but on sunny days and in windless conditions one can have the most exciting lake fishing for grayling. Fishing pressure is low here, as many are put off by the size of these lakes and the usually unremitting wind. However, if one gets to know these lakes well and studies the map carefully, you can usually find some spot relatively unaffected by the wind and where the fish are to be found. One quickly discovers the value of reconnaissance here and time spent exploring is worthwhile. An unprepared day-trip can end easily result in frustration. For me, just being there is enough. Maybe that's why I never seem to blank there.

The lakes of Hodalen are about 1000m above sea level, which is the perfect altitude for grayling. The water is deep, icy cold and crystal clear and most of the year covered with ice. In the past, there was quite high netting pressure in summer, but stocks were never seriously endangered and when the netting stopped many years ago the population of grayling, white fish, pike and perch increased rapidly.

Occasionally, one is rewarded with a bonus from the lakes. My biggest-ever perch on the fly was caught there. More than once, I've seen huge fish hunting close to the shore but couldn't figure out what species they were. My attention was sometimes drawn to the enormous splashes of these hunting fish. At first I thought they were pike, but a closer look showed me my error. I knew that monster trout had been caught in the past. I call them the ghosts of Hodalen! Wildlife in the area is a bit shy but around midnight you can often see reindeer and elk crossing the lakes against the unbelievable colours of the midsummer night sky.

The lakes of Hodalen are a perfect place to experiment with the Once and Away. Although the lakes are deep, in some places there are shallow bays and shores where one can wade out more than a 100m from the shore. The third year I visited Hodalen, I discovered a place where the lake is narrower and quite shallow. There is also a little current. This place turned out to be a real hotspot and has been captured by one of my good friends in a wonderful oil painting which hangs in our living room.

For some years, I concentrated on the steepest drop-offs and I was lucky to find some good places. If, however, you fish the shallow bays and wade carefully, grayling and white fish will come in quite close to you by the hundreds in search for food. You can clearly see them feeding on the bottom and in the surface. At one particular place, you can see them feeding in big shoals just two or three metres from the shore. Wind lanes are often found where the shallows begin and these can produce some awesome fishing as well. It's in places like these that I mainly use my Once and Away. You quickly discover how effective this pattern is if you allow the wind to give it some extra movement. I like to fish this pattern very close to a wind lane, allowing the wind to bring it close to the feeding fish. Another advantage of the Once and Away is its visibility at distance. At times, the grayling suck the fly down so gently from the surface that there is almost no disturbance. If you can't see the fly, chances are it hasn't sunk on its own but has been taken quietly by a fish and you need to get a move on and set the hook.

Although this fly was designed especially for still water fishing, it works well in the inlets, outlets and the rivers connecting the lakes. Most of the time I give some extra action to the Once and Away: tiny movements of the rod tip to make the fly move on the surface. Just a little wake around the fly seems to tempt the most selective fish. I don't know why, but that's how it is. People often ask me what the Once and Away really imitates. I'm afraid I don't know that either! I only know that this pattern works well when midges are hatching. A personal theory I have is that while midges are actually quite small, when they hatch they look much larger than they really are. Maybe that's the secret behind this fly."

Piet Weeda

Piet Weeda is one of Holland's best CDC tyers. His functional patterns were developed for the trout of Lake Oostvoorne (a large lake that came into being when Holland's Delta plan was realised) and for his trout and grayling fishing in Germany and Austria.

Right: Piet Weeda fishing in Austria

1. CDC BLUE DUN

This is an effective mayfly imitation. The yellow ribbing is an important detail that certainly seems to contribute to its attractiveness. The hackle of deer hair tips also seems quite special, making the fly slightly more rugged and increasing its buoyancy.

Hook: TMC 902 BL, size 14—18

Thread: Benecchi 12/0 black

Tail: Coq de León fibres

Body: Twisted CDC feather, MP style

Ribbing: Dirty yellow Lureflash thread

Wing: Bunch of CDC fibres

Hackle: Fine tips of deer hair, twisted in dubbing loop

2. CDC SPENT SPINNER

This is a great pattern when female mayflies are fluttering over the water to lay their eggs.

Hook: TMC 902 BL, size 12—16

Thread: Benecchi 12/0 brown

Tail: Coq de León fibres

Body: Twisted red CDC feather

Ribbing: Extra fine gold tinsel

Wing: Tips of CDC feathers

Hackle: Fine tips of deer hair, twisted in dubbing loop

3. CDC SPENT

After egg laying, ephemerid spinners collapse on the water surface and die. In quiet water, fish can quietly cruise along just under the surface mopping up the spent spinners simply by opening their mouths. A small strip of Polycelon over the thorax increases the visibility to the angler.

Hook: TMC 5230, size 12—16

Thread: Benecchi 12/0 light brown

Tail: Brown cock hackle fibres

Body: Super dry fly dubbing colour orange/brown

Wing: Tips of CDC feathers or just a small feather

Thorax: Strip of 3mm yellow Polycelon

4. O.V. (OORTVOORNE) LAKE SCUD

Hook: TMC 2312, size 10—14

Thread: Benecchi 12/0 olive

Tail: Wood duck

Body: Polycelon olive

Legs: Olive CDC fibres

Ribbing: Nylon 0.15mm colour brown

Back: Polycelon olive

Piet Weeda CDC patterns, clockwise from top left: OV Lake Scud, CDC Spent, CDC Spent Spinner, CDC Blue Dun.

My Last Evening on the Lenne
by Piet Weeda

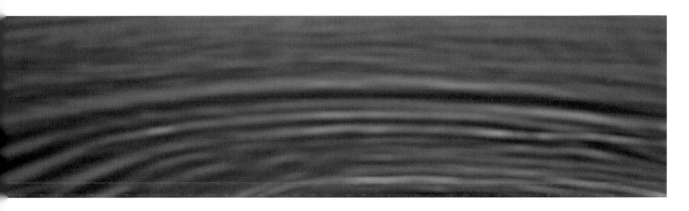

"The CDC Blue Dun has done incredibly well for me on Germany's river Lenne. On several days, we had little difficulty in catching forty or fifty trout and grayling. It is a great shame that the Lenne has been ruined by pollution and cormorants! In the spring of 1999, I fished the Lenne once more, but that was it for me. The Lenne is conveniently close to the Netherlands and I do hope it can recover so that we can fish it again some day.

On the last evening fishing, before our group set off for home, I didn't feel like putting on my chest waders again. One of my friends stepped into the water at the very spot I had intended to start fishing myself, so I sat down to watched him for a while. After a bit, he waded off downstream, and I was surprised to see some good grayling feeding on the spot he had just left. The size 12 CDC Blue Dun I knotted on seemed rather large, but I had run out of smaller flies. It hardly mattered! In about two hours, I caught 17 grayling between 36 and 46cm."

Leon Links

The author Leon Links fishing the River Kyll near Marlberg, Germany. *Photo: Hans Van Klinken*

1. L PUPA

This fly should be fished in the film or just below the surface.

Hook: Partridge K 14ST, size10–18

Thread: Black 8/0

Body: Yellow, green or brown Irisé dubbing, or CDC dubbing

Wing: CDC palmered (in dubbing loop)

2. DUCK CADDIS

This is my favourite caddis pattern for flat water conditions.

Hook: TMC 5230, size 10—16

Thread: Black 8/0

Body: Green Fly-Rite dubbing

Wing: About four pairs of CDC feathers, matched for size and colour

Hackle: Chocolate dun cock hackle clipped underneath for low profile

3. L CADDIS

A buoyant fly for riffles and choppy water.

Hook: TMC 100, size 10—16

Thread: Black 8/0

Wing and body: Fibres of approximately five CDC feathers

Antennae (optional): Two CDC quills

Tying instruction for the L Caddis:

1. Make a foundation with the tying thread and tie in a bunch of CDC fibres at the hook bend.

2. Form a dubbing loop at the point where the fibres are mounted. Close the loop with a turn of thread around the base of the loop. Prepare two CDC feathers in two paper clamps (as shown in Chapter 6)

3. Wax the loop lightly, insert the CDC feathers and spin the loop to trap the CDC fibres.

4. Now wind the dubbing loop up the shank.

5. Tie in on top of the shank, just behind the hook eye, two strands of Uni Stretch and the optional antennae.

6. Pull back the Uni Stretch between the antennae, dividing them, and tie down.

7. Form a second CDC fibre string.

8. Wind the string around the second half of the shank, pulling the fibres up and back all the time, so as not to over-wind them.

9. Tie off and trim the feathers into a caddis-shape.

4. L NYMPH

I describe the L nymph as a 'generic' nymph pattern.

Hook: TMC 200, size 8–16, with lead wire windings
Thread: Black 8/0
Tail: Brown CDC fibres
Abdomen: Brown CDC dubbing, copper wire
Thorax: Brown rabbit fur and brown CDC fibres
Wing case: Strip of turkey feather

5. L COMPARA

My favourite dun (and spent) imitation in riffles.

Hook: TMC 5230, size 10–16
Thread: Black 8/0
Tail: Coq de León fibres
Abdomen: CDC feather wound Marc Petitjean style (matching colour)
Thorax: CDC dubbing same colour
Wings: Two middle size CDC feathers with supple stem, hackled

6. L SPENT

Same materials as L Compara

Tying instruction **for the L Compara:**

1. Make a foundation and tie in 6 to 10 fibres from the Coq de León hackle. Take a length of Uni Stretch, and trap it at the hook bend. Twist the material between the fingers and divide the tail into two equal bunches.

2. Take a long CDC feather and tie it in by the tip.

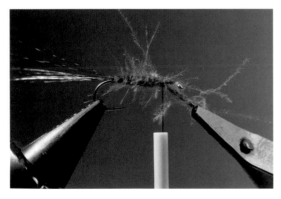

3. Wind the CDC body (twisting the feather after each turn) to about a third of the shank-length from the eye. Tie the remaining feather part firmly and clip off.

4. Tie in two CDC feathers by the stem, concave side facing away from the shank: one just behind the hook eye, the second between the first feather and the body. Bring the thread between the feathers.

5 & 6 Take three or four turns of the first feather, tie off the feather, trim the excess and bring the thread towards the body. Take about the same number of turns of the second feather, tie off and trim the excess. Pull the fibres up and secure them into position with turns of thread wound behind and in front of the fibres. Dub a thin 'noodle' of CDC dubbing (same colour as abdomen) onto the thread and wind thorax behind and in front of the fibres.

7. Form a neat thread head, whip finish and trim the thread. Pull the CDC fibres to either side into the Comparadun shape.

8. The finished L Compara, viewed from above.

To tie the L Spent, follow steps 1. – 5 . as for the L Compara (above) and then finish the fly as shown below

9. Form two spent wings by pulling half of the fibres to one side of the shank and the other half to the other side. Secure with figure-of-eight turns of thread. Dub CDC fibres onto the thread (same colour as abdomen) and wind on turns so as to cover the thread windings.

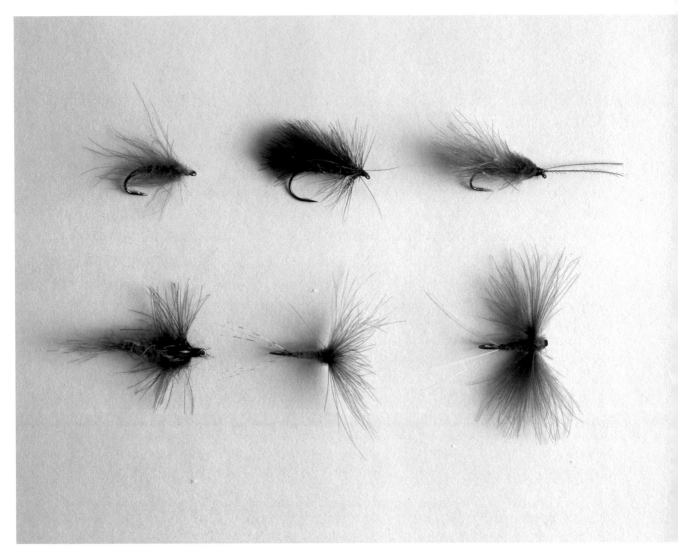

Leon Links' patterns, clockwise from top left: L Pupa, Duck Caddis, L Caddis, L Spent, L Compara, L Nymph

Paolo Jaia

A Roman by birth, Paolo works for Italy's leading independent TV network. Paolo is also a keen amateur entomologist. In 1991 he founded May Fly Productions, Italy's first production company specialising in fly-fishing videos. From the beginning, he has enjoyed the collaboration of his partner, Lidia di Lorenzo, herself an angler and photographer. Paolo has fished the best known waters in Italy and the rest of Europe and he spends long periods every year fishing in the United States. A member of the Federation of Fly Fishers, he has taught at Piero Letizia's 'Advanced Fly Casting School' since its inauguration.

Paolo Jaia. *Photo by Lidia di Lorenzo*

1. S W CADDIS

CDC dubbing makes this fly buoyant. It is suited to chalkstreams and large rivers with relatively slow currents. In the larger sizes and in grey shades, it is effective during hatches of the big grey sedge Odontocerum albicorne, which occurs on the rivers of central Italy.

Hook: TMC 100, size 8—18
Thread: Benecchi Ultra Fine XXF - brown
Abdomen: Benecchi natural CDC dubbing
Thorax: Benecchi dark CDC dubbing
Wings: Hen pheasant feather section lacquered
Antennae: Two hackle quills
Head: Brown tying thread

5. HJ 15

A classic caddis for trout and grayling in choppy waters, or large streams. To make the fly more visible in the evening, Paolo adds a tuft of white Float Vis on the head of the fly.

Hook: TMC 100, size 10—18

Thread: Benecchi Ultra Fine XXF – brown

Abdomen: Two natural CDC feathers twisted and wrapped around the shank of the hook

Thorax: Black CDC dubbing

Wings: Deer hair and two CDC feathers wrapped around the shank of the hook

6. GLF CDC

This pattern was directly inspired by the late Gary LaFontaine's famous caddis imitation.

This version is a floating fly and constructed entirely with CDC.

Hook: TMC 100, size 16—22

Thread: Benecchi Ultra Fine XXF - black

Under body: Yellow CDC feather wrapped around the shank of the hook

Over body: Two black CDC feathers tied as a loop over and under the body

Thorax: Black CDC dubbing

Wings: Two black CDC feathers

Hackle: One black CDC feather

7. SPIDER CADDIS

An effective variant of the classic spider fly.

Hook: TMC 2457, size 10—16

Thread: Benecchi Ultra Fine XXF - black

Body: Unwaxed dental floss dyed yellow, dyed green by Pantone marker
             and then lacquered

Rib: Thin copper wire

Thorax: Benecchi New Dub - olive

Hackle: One partridge feather and one CDC feather

Head: Black bead 2.8mm dia.

8. PINK KILLER

This Diptera imitation is a lethal little grayling catcher. It is Paolo's version of the classic 'Scarpantibus' pattern, usually tied with pink floss and a black hackle. The little beads give the body translucency and the tuft of CDC keeps it floating just under the surface.

Hook: TMC 100, size 18—24

Thread: Benecchi Ultra Fine XXF - black

Body: Peacock fibres and one to two little pink beads (according to the size of the hook)

Wings: Tuft of natural or white CDC fibres

9. G B QUILL

This is another pattern incorporating a small bead. It works well in sizes 14-20 during Ephemeroptera hatches, or in larger sizes as a general stimulator pattern.

Hook: TMC 100, size 14—20

Thread: Benecchi Ultra Fine XXF - black

Tail: Furnace hackle fibres tied very short

Abdomen: Furnace quill dyed green with Pantone marker and then lacquered

Thorax: One little green bead – peacock fibres

Wings: Tuft of natural CDC fibres

10. NERA MAYFLY

The Nera river, which flows through the region of Umbria in central Italy, is very rich in insects. This pattern is practically indispensable during hatches of *Ephemera danica* on this river.

Hook: TMC 2487, size 8—10

Thread: Benecchi Ultra Fine XXF - brown

Abdomen: Extended body tube - medium mayfly, dark sulphur. The segmentation and body markings of the natural are imitated using Pantone marker

Thorax: New Dub Fine - yellow

Hackle: One Benecchi Hyper select khaki CDC feather

Wings: Four CDC feathers tied upright and split - two on each side - with five or six pheasant tail fibres

Head: New Dub Fine - yellow, coloured black on top with Pantone marker

N.B. The emerger version of this pattern is almost the same, but the four CDC feathers are tied to form loops.

Antonio Rinaldin

An enthusiastic member of the Milan Fly Angling Club, Antonio has been flyfishing and tying flies since the early 1980s. He spends many hours at his workbench tying everything from small dry flies to bass poppers and salt-water lures and flies for salmon and steelhead.

Antonio has practised 'catch-and-release' for years, but also enjoys capturing fishing highlights on film. He lives outside Milan with his wife and daughter.

Antonio Rinaldin's CDC patterns, clockwise from top left: Tricolor CDC Caddis, Skater Caddis, Tuft Caddis, HW Compara, Dump CDC and Winter Cotton..

1. H W COMPARA

This is an imitation of an emerging ephemerid. The CDC loop makes the pattern visible and buoyant.

Hook: TMC 100, size 14—16

Thread: Brown

Tail: John Betts Microfibetts fibres

Rib: The butt ends of the tail material (Microfibetts)

Abdomen: Caddis Emerger dubbing - rusty

Thorax: Caddis Emerger dubbing - rusty

Wings: Tuft of deer hair, split by a loop of natural or white CDC

2. TRICOLOR CDC CADDIS

An interesting caddis imitation that Antonio uses on summer evenings on the river Adda in Valtellina.

Hook: TMC 100, size 12—14

Thread: Orange

Body: One Benecchi CDC Devaux feather (No. 04 - brown), twisted and wound on the whole hook shank, with another CDC Devaux feather (No. 18 - salmon pink), palmered on top

Collar: Two turns of white CDC feather

Wings: Natural mallard feather tip

3. WINTER COTTON

Emerging ephemera imitation used on small or medium streams in autumn or winter.

Hook: TMC 100, size 12—16

Thread: Grey

Tail: Natural mallard

Abdomen: Dubbing of grey hare's hair

Thorax: Dubbing of CDC fibres

Wings: Natural CDC feather wound and pulled upright

4. TUFT CADDIS

An effective caddis imitation for medium or big rivers. Antonio has used this fly for many years on the river Sesia.

Hook: TMC 100, size l2—14
Thread: Pale yellow
Abdomen: Apple green Caucci/Nastasi dubbing
Wings: Two spotted and two natural grey CDC feathers (alternate), wound tight and pulled upright
Thorax: CDC dubbing

33. SKATER CADDIS

This clever caddis imitation skates on the surface: the ends of the CDC feathers, protruding on either side of the thorax, throw out a nice wake. It is a very good lake pattern too.

Hook: TMC 200R, size 12—14
Thread: Pale yellow
Abdomen: Caddis Emerger dubbing (No. 19 - March Brown)
Rib: Crystal Flash - pearl
Wings: Two natural grey CDC feathers, leaving the two quills ends sticking out
Wing case: CDC feathers
Thorax: CDC dubbing

34. DUMP CDC

A tiny stimulator. Very good on small or medium streams, especially for grayling.

Hook: TMC 100, size 14—16
Thread: Black
Abdomen: Red or green flat tinsel
Back: Two natural grey CDC feathers tied forward
Thorax: Peacock fibres
Wings: Tips of same feathers used for the back

Gigi Goldoni

Gigi Goldoni was born in Formigine and lives in Vignola, near Modena, Italy. He has been a fly fisherman since he was 18 and is an expert on dry and wet flies in fast flowing waters. His speciality is upstream fishing with nymphs. A skilled flytyer and inventor of tying equipment and materials, Gigi created New Dub: an extraordinary innovative material suited to a wide range of flytying application. He founded the Modena Fly Fishing Club and has worked with Giorgio Benecchi since 1989. Gigi is currently the manager of Flies & Lies in Modena.

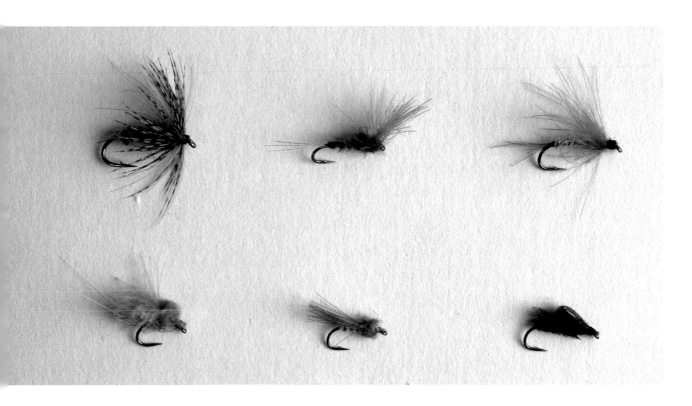

Gigi Goldoni's Italian CDC variations, clockwise from top left: Emergente, Temolo, WG Emerger, Terrestre, Tutto, Extended body CDC Emerger.

1. EMERGENTE

This emerging ephemerid imitation works extremely well in small streams, fished at very short ranges of four to five metres if you help it float with the tip of the rod held high. It's very good as a nymph too, especially in lakes. It can be weighted with lead wire, a gold bead, or a little shot on the leader.

Hook: TMC 376, size 12—16

Thread: Benecchi Ultra Fine XXF - brown

Abdomen: Natural brown opossum dubbing

Rib: New Dub - fine gold

Thorax: Squirrel fur dyed olive

Hackle: One Benecchi khaki Hyper select CDC feather and one brown partridge feather

Head: Brown tying thread

2. TEMOLO (GRAYLING)

A small ephemerid pattern for selective fish. It has been very successful on the rivers of Valtellina, especially for grayling.

Hook: TMC 100, size 18

Thread: Benecchi Ultra Fine XXF - brown

Tail: Light dun hackle fibres

Abdomen: Benecchi CDC dubbing - khaki

Rib: One moose mane fibre, tied in by the tip

Thorax: Benecchi CDC dubbing - black

Wings: One Benecchi Hyper select CDC feather - khaki

Head: Brown tying thread

3. W G EMERGER

The WG Emerger is an effective fly during ephemerid hatches and is useful for stimulating takes from selective fish.

Hook: Tiemco TMC 100, size 16

Thread: Benecchi Ultra Fine XXF - brown

Tail: Benecchi CDC fibres - khaki

Abdomen: Bleached peacock quill from the eye of the feather

Rib: Fine copper wire

Thorax: Benecchi CDC dubbing - khaki

Wings: Hen pheasant feather section, lacquered

Head: Brown tying thread

4. TUTTO

A good Stone fly imitation when choices are hard. It is often difficult to see, so it is advisable to put a little strike indicator on the leader.

Hook: TMC 100, size 18—20

Thread: Benecchi Ultra Fine XXF - brown

Abdomen: Bleached peacock quill from the eye of the feather

Rib: Fine copper wire

Thorax: Benecchi CDC dubbing - khaki

Wings: One Benecchi CDC feather - khaki

Head: Brown tying thread

5. EXTENDED BODY CDC EMERGER

This is an excellent imitation of an emerging ephemerid. For grayling, it is better to omit the Microfibbett tail, which might impede the fly's entry into the fish's rather small mouth. Use New Dub for the extended body.

Hook: TMC 2487, size 18

Thread: Benecchi Ultra Fine XXF - sand

Tail: Two light dun Microfibetts

Abdomen: New Dub fine: the first part tied in as extended body, the remainder wrapped round the hook shank to form the thorax

Wings: One 'oiler puff' CDC feather, forming a little loop wing

Head: Sand-coloured tying thread

6. TERRESTRE

A good small terrestrial imitation, especially when fished under riverbank trees in summer.

Hook: TMC 100, size 18

Thread: Benecchi Ultra Fine XXF - brown

Body: Peacock fibres from the eye of the feather

Wings: One black CDC feather forming a little loop wing

Head: Brown tying thread

Marco Feliciani

Marco lives and works in his native Milan. He has been flyfishing since 1977 and ties around 7,000 flies every year. A man of many interests, Marco experiments with new materials to create innovative and alluring imitations. He flyfishes for just about anything that will take a fly, including trout, bass, pike, grayling and barbel, mainly in the rivers and lakes of northern and central Italy. He has fished in much of continental Europe, in North America and in Cuba.

Marco Feliciani's CDC patterns, clockwise from top left: Bitch Flats, Loop Sedge, M-Bee, Little Stone Fly, Flash Midge, Caddis Emerger.

1. BITCH FLATS

Attractive for bonefish, small barracuda, red snapper, mutton snapper and permit. The lead wire in the curve of the hook makes the fly sink fast and inverted, which helps prevent snagging algae. Bitch Flats are almost the 'official' flies at the 'Casa Batida' Lodge in Cuba's Cayo Largo.

Hook: TMC 411 S, size 4—6, weighted with lead wire
Thread: Benecchi ultra strong
Eyes: Nylon 0.40, burnt and coloured with Pantone Marker
Body: Benecchi iridescent thread, coated with epoxy
Legs: Two CDC feathers, the same colour as the body; eight to ten Crystal Flash fibres and a CDC feather wrapped hackle-fashion

Note: Marco ties this fly in silver, yellow and pink.

2. LOOP SEDGE

The use of lots of CDC gives this caddis a very solid appearance, but without the hardness or rigidity of other materials. It is a good fly for medium to large rivers and chalkstreams and on lakes.

Hook: TMC 2312, size10—14
Thread: Benecchi ultra fine thread XXF
Body: Two CDC feathers, trimmed
Wings: Three long-fibred CDC feathers
Hackle: One CDC feather
Head: Benecchi CDC dubbing
Antennae: Two moose fibres

Note: effective colours are brown, olive, black and grey.

3. CADDIS EMERGER

Hook: TMC 2488, size 12—14
Thread: Benecchi ultra fine XXF
Body: Two CDC feathers, trimmed
Hackle: One CDC feather
Head: Benecchi CDC Dubbing
Antennae: Two moose fibres

Note: best colours are yellow, brown, olive and grey

4. CDC STONE FLY NYMPH

An effective stone fly nymph. The CDC body makes it look realistic. The two gold beads make this a fast sinking pattern.

Hook:	TMC 3761, size 10—14
Thread:	Benecchi ultra fine XXF
Tail:	Two turkey or goose biots
Abdomen:	Two CDC feathers, trimmed and shaped
Thorax:	Two gold beads of different diameter: 2.5mm and 3.0mm.
Hackle:	One CDC feather wrapped around the gold beads

Note: best colours are brown, olive, black and grey

5. M – BEE

Tied with CDC only, this is a very effective fly during the middle of the day in summer, on rivers of moderate current or in mountain lakes.

Hook:	TMC 2312, size 10—12
Thread:	Benecchi ultra fine XXF - black
Body:	Black and yellow CDC feathers, trimmed and shaped
Wings:	Two white CDC feathers
Hackle:	One blue-grey Benecchi CDC Devaux feather

6. APT

The classic Pheasant Tail Nymph fully deserves its reputation, but Marco's variation, containing a gold bead and CDC fibres, makes it even more interesting. The fly is dedicated to the famous Italian caster and fly-fisher, Alberto Giovannelli (APT = Alberto Pheasant Tail).

Hook:	TMC 3769, size12—14
Thread:	Benecchi ultra fine XXF - brown
Tail:	Four to five cock pheasant tail fibres
Abdomen:	Same fibres from the tail
Rib and Thorax:	Copper wire, diameter 0.14mm to 0.16mm
Hackle:	One brown CDC feather
Head:	Gold bead dia. 2.5mm – 3.0mm.

7. LITTLE STONE FLY

Used in smaller sizes this is a fly for trout and grayling on Italian rivers.

Larger sizes come in useful on the mountain lakes.

Hook: TMC 2312, size 14—20

Thread: Benecchi ultra fine XXF - dark brown

Body: Ligas dubbing No. 049

Wings: Two goose or turkey biots dyed black or dark grey

Hackle: One dark grey CDC feather

Head: Dubbing as for body

8. FLASH MIDGE

A fantasy chironomid or diptera imitation which has proved very good for grayling in slow water, or for larger trout in mountain lakes.

Hook: TMC 921, size 14—18

Thread: Benecchi ultra fine XXF - black or brown

Abdomen: Three to four pearl Crystal Flash fibres

Thorax: Two peacock fibres

Wings: Five to six pearl Crystal Flash fibres and a tuft of CDC fibres dyed black

Elie Beerten

One of Belgium's prominent flyfishers, Elie Beerten ties some extremely subtle CDC flies to fish reservoirs in Belgium and England, the great loughs of Ireland and the wonderful rivers and streams in the Belgian Ardennes and the German Eifel.

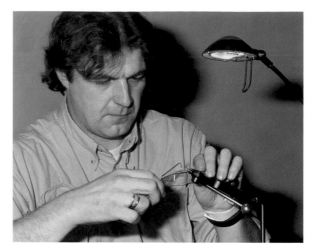

Elie Beerten concentrating at the vice at a Belgian Flyfishing Fair.
Rudy van Duijnhoven

1. NO BODY

A low-water dry fly containing just a few trigger elements. Flies with a minimum of tying material are sometimes necessary to tempt selective fish. Elie's No Bodies are tied on golden hooks to give an attractive yellowish glitter to the fly, matching the colour of many emergers. The thorax is actually a support to keep the main wing up high. No Bodies tied without body and tail are equally effective.

Hook: TMC 2487/2487 G, size 16—18
Thread: 8/0 Light olive, or any matching colour
Body: Tying thread
Tail: Approximately five cock hackle fibres, matching colour
Thorax: CDC feather trimmed short
Wing: Fibres of the same CDC feather tied back over thorax, stem clipped out.

2. W.W. (WEE WHISPER)

The Wee Whisper is a most delicate dun imitation. It is hard to beat when fish, particularly grayling or choosy larger trout, are after specific small dun species.

Hook: TMC 921, size 18—22
Thread: 8/0 light olive, or colour to match the hatch
Tail: CDC fibres for extra buoyancy
Wings: CDC fibres of two feathers (tips clipped out) divided in two by means of a
            figure-of-eight whipping

1. Make a foundation with the tying thread. Clip out the tips of two medium size CDC feathers. Put the feathers together and tie them in by the tips of the stem, where the wings are to stand out from the body.

2. Clip off the waste ends of the feathers, tie in a bunch of CDC fibres for the tail and wind a slim body.

3. Divide the wing fibres with the thread.

4. Erect the wings and secure in a V-shape position, with a few more turns of thread.

3. ADULT SEDGE 1

This is an easy-to-tie, high floating, very visible and effective sedge imitation.

Hook: TMC 100, size 12—16

Thread: Grey 8/0

Body: Cream CDC dubbing

Wing: Two to four CDC feather tips (depending on size and quality).

           The alternating light and dark fibres produce a beautiful mottled effect

Hackle: CDC feather

Antennae (optional):   Fibres of duck flank feather

Elie Beerten's CDC patterns, clockwise from top left: No Body, Damsel, WW, Adult Sedge 2, Adult Sedge 1.

A fine grayling for Elie Beerten from a smaller river in the German Eiffel. *Patrick Daniels*

4. ADULT SEDGE 2

This pattern sits quite low in the water, but floats well. It is a fair representation of several caddis species. It is effective when fished dead-drift, but skitters easily over the surface on its deer hair legs when this is required. It is based on a Scandinavian sedge pattern, in which the deer hair wing has been replaced by CDC.

Hook: TMC 100, size 12–16
Thread: 8/0 light brown
Body: Yellow brown dubbing
Sedge wing: About six bunches of CDC, alternating light and dark fibres to produce a mottled image
Legs: Very fine deer hair
Antennae: Two squirrel hairs

5. DAMSEL

This is a fantastic fly in summer, when damsels skim along the banks. Trout sometimes jump high out of the water to intercept these insects in their mating dance. The CDC Damsel must be presented and fished close to the bank. Trout can attack it viciously.

Hook: TMC 2487, size 10
Thread: 6/0 Blue
Abdomen: Twisted electric blue micro tinsel (Uni thread)
Thorax: Polypropylene blue
Wing: Two CDC feather tips, stems clipped out

Clive Perkins

Probably the best-known CDC pattern in the British Isles was devised by Clive Perkins, a stillwater specialist and a keen competition flyfisher. Today, it is almost impossible to imagine stillwater flyfishing without his Shuttlecock.

SHUTTLECOCK CDC

Hook: Kamasan B170, size 12
Body: Cock pheasant tail feather fibres
Rib: Fine silver, gold or copper wire or fine monofilament
Wing: CDC feathers

Evolution of the Shuttlecock CDC
by Clive Perkins

"I have always been fascinated by the concept of dry fly fishing and, as so many anglers before me, set out to invent the magic fly that would always catch fish. It's an impossible goal, of course, but we spend a great deal of time chasing the elusive grail and have a lot of fun experimenting in the process.

One of the most successful semi-submerged buzzer patterns is Goddard's Suspender Buzzer, with its polystyrene or Ethafoam ball head. Unfortunately, this fly is not visible to the angler at any distance from the boat: the fly sits so low in the water that the 'suspender' ball is barely visible and most of the time definite takes are only detected when the fly line is pulled from your hands. Trying to pre-empt the fish by striking at swirls results in the fish that come short being spooked by one's attempts to strike. Another problem with the Suspender Buzzer is that it tends to spin and twist the leader.

Since CDC had been used as a buoyancy aid for river flies for a long time, I decided to try and develop a fly similar to the Suspender Buzzer, but using CDC instead of foam. Initially, I tied the CDC in at the top of the hook, shuttlecock-style, then tried various combinations of body materials and different styles and weights of hooks to imitate a chironomid trapped in the surface film. The prototypes were tested in glasses of water. However, the conditions in a glass of water on my tying bench are a long way from those found out on the reservoir. Initially, I tied far too much CDC into the fly.

Clive Perkins' CDC Shuttlecock series. Top row flies tied by Clive Perkins. Second row: four Shuttlecock variations tied by Paul Canning (fly on the left is the Black Spot), Chris Howitt and Elie Beerten.

Continuing my experiments at the reservoir, I tied one of the prototypes onto a leader let it drop onto the water very close to the boat, so that I could watch it and see how it sat in the water. I soon discovered that if there was too much CDC on the fly, it would lie almost flat on the surface. However, as I progressively trimmed away small amounts of the CDC, the fly would sit more vertically in the water.

The secret was to get the correct weight and size of hook; then to use the correct body material for the hook and then to use just enough CDC to keep the fly sitting vertically in the water. I found that the best combination was to use a Kamasan B170 size 12, with the body dressed with cock pheasant tail fibres ribbed with either very fine wire (silver, gold or copper), or very fine nylon monofilament. The ribbing is really mainly to improve the durability of the herl body.

Because I was doing a great deal of competition fly fishing at the time, it was very important that any fly I used met the strict rules governing the size of fly permitted under 'International Rules'. This would normally allow me to have the CDC protruding around 6mm to 8mm above the eye of the hook. The main advantage of using CDC 'shuttlecock style' is that it makes the fly extremely visible to the angler at range. When a trout head and tails over the fly and it disappears, you can be pretty sure that the fish has taken it and you can strike with confidence.

Since my initial experiments about nine years ago (1992) there have been too many variations of this concept to mention: new hook patterns and weights and new materials. New imitations have been developed for fully dressed buzzer imitations; short dressed patterns; snail imitations; corixae and even fry patterns. I find that the Shuttlecock is best fished as a single fly, on a leader of approximately 15 feet (4.5m) long and used to target individual feeding fish cruising in the top layer. In summary, I believe that the Shuttlecock's success is due partly to the profile of the fly hanging vertically in the water, which makes it more visible to the trout, and partly to its visibility to the angler at range."

René Harrop

René is a resident of Idaho who has fished Henry's Fork and other waters of the Yellowstone area since the age of nine. Since 1968, René and his wife, Bonnie, have run the 'House of Harrop': a fly-tying service and supplier of tying materials. They were joined by daughter Leslie and son Shayne, who are both exceptional tyers. The Harrops

René Harrop fishing the famous Henry's Fork in Idaho, USA.

specialise in tying specific imitations for hatches, world-wide. They have customers in more than a dozen foreign countries, as well as from all over the USA.

In the early 1990s, René was one of a few fly fishers to introduce and popularise CDC in the USA. In the July 1991 issue of *Fly Fisherman,* René published an excellent article on CDC. It was featured on the magazine's cover as *'Cul de Canard Feathers: A Fly-tying Revolution'.* It is interesting to learn about his findings when fishing CDC imitations of midges, duns, caddis flies and terrestrials in their various stages.

Thoughts on CDC

by René Harrop

"Although I have relied strongly upon feathers from waterfowl since the mid-1950s, it is only in the past dozen or so years that CDC has played a part in my own flytying. Despite this relatively short acquaintance, CDC has established itself as one of my favourite materials for imitative flytying.

On the Henry's Fork, which flows nearby, only good presentation of credible imitations will bring sustained results. More than any other material, CDC allows me to duplicate the appearance, behaviour and position of floating or partially submerged insects. The flotational benefits of CDC are well known. It is my opinion that overdressing an imitative fly is the most common reason for refusal. On pressured waters, trout are easily deterred by clumsy, overdressed attempts at imitation. Amazingly small amounts of CDC will give adequate support on these slow clear currents: precisely where selectivity is at it highest.

From the beginning I have treated CDC feathers as though they were hackle tips when winging dry flies or emerging patterns. Typically, two feathers are used for wings, although one feather will often suffice for extremely small caddis or midge styles. I sort the CDC according to the size of fly I intend to tie, saving the longest feathers for Drakes and other large imitations. Fibres stripped from the centre stem work nicely for legs, tails and antennae.

Much has been made of CDC's ability to trap air bubbles, but I am not certain this feature triggers a positive response from trout. I am convinced, however, that the yielding nature of CDC fibres gives subtle movement to the fly. I believe this contributes to a more lifelike appearance than do stiffer materials such as deer hair.

The test of any fly is its ability to fool the fish. From my experience, well designed and properly constructed CDC flies easily hold their own among the world's most successful patterns. Despite its popularity in other countries, CDC has yet to receive full approval here in the U.S.A. Perhaps expectations have been too high and people have failed to understand the material properly. No fly - however good - can cancel out poor casting skills. Similarly, a poorly tied fly will seldom dupe educated trout, regardless of its components.

Such is my confidence in these remarkable little feathers, that I rarely have anything other than a CDC pattern on my tippet these days! I don't say that I can fool every trout I encounter. Fly-fishing is just not like that. However, I believe my chances are as good with a CDC fly as with anything else. I have no doubt that CDC is here to stay and that its popularity can only increase with time."

1. HENRY'S FORK CADDIS EMERGER

Hook: TMC 100, size to match natural

Thread: 8/0 waxed

Tail: Three to four Caddis green CDC fibres

Abdomen: Caddis green goose or turkey biot

Wings: Two CDC feather tips mounted in the normal wing position

Legs: Partridge flank feather fibres tied in at the throat

Head: Caddis Emerger dubbing - black

2. BLACK FLYING ANT

Hook: TMC 100, size to match natural

Thread: 8/0 waxed

Abdomen: Harrop black fine natural dubbing

Stabilizers: Two moose hairs, one on each side of abdomen

Wings: Two CDC feather tips

Hackle: Black cock hackle short in the fibre

Head: as abdomen

3. GRAY MIDGE ADULT

Hook: TMC 100, size to match natural

Thread: 8/0 waxed

Abdomen: Canada goose biot

Wings: Two CDC feather tips arranged to flare away from each other

Thorax: Muskrat grey fine natural dubbing

Hackle: Grizzle cock hackle short in the fibre

Head: Grey tying thread

4. PMD BIOT DUN

Hook: TMC 100, size to match natural

Thread: 8/0 waxed

Tail: Two CDC fibres tied over about four Coq de León hackle fibres

Abdomen: PMD goose or turkey biot

Wings: Two CDC feather tips arranged to flare away from each other

Legs: Butts of the CDC wings tied back along the sides of the fly, clipped even with the rear of the abdomen

Thorax: PMD fine natural dubbing

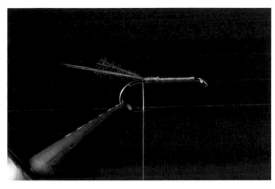

1. Wind a foundation of touching turns. Wrap a wisp of about five cock hackle fibres and add a few shorter CDC fibres on top of the tail.

2. Erect the tail slightly with a turn of thread under the base. Tie in the biot by the tip.

3. Wind the body and leave approximately one-third of the shank bare (behind the eye).

4. Tie in two CDC feathers where the biot body ends, tips flaring away from each other. Spin dubbing material onto the thread, but sparsely.

5. Wind some wraps of dubbing behind the feathers to form the thorax and erect the wings. Wind some wraps directly in front of the wings.

6. Pull the feather stems back along the body on either side. Wind the thorax with the dubbing, at the same time positioning the legs.

7. Whip finish and clip the legs even with the rear of the abdomen.

5. LITTLE OLIVE STONE FLY

Hook: TMC 100, size to match natural

Thread: 8/0 waxed

Tail: Red marabou fibres

Abdomen: Goose biot dyed red

Wing: Two CDC feathers tied in flat over the abdomen and tail

Thorax: Harrop fine natural dubbing - light olive

Legs: Butts of the CDC wings tied back along the sides of the fly,
            clipped halfway along the abdomen

6. BROWN DRAKE LAST CHANCE CRIPPLE

Hook: TMC 100, size 10

Thread: 8/0 waxed

Tail: Barred lemon wood duck

Abdomen: Goose biot dyed dark brown

Thorax: Tannish yellow dubbing

Hackle: Dark brown cock hackle

Wing: Two natural brown CDC feathers

7. CDC PALMERED CADDIS ADULT

Hook: TMC 100, size 12

Thread: 8/0 waxed

Abdomen: Dark tan dubbing

Thorax: Same as abdomen

Hackle: Dark brown cock hackle

Wing: Two natural brown CDC feathers

René Harrop's CDC patterns, top row CDC Palmered Caddis Adult, Black Flying Ant, PMD Biot Dun. Middle fly: Brown Drake Last Chance Cripple. Bottom row Little Olive Stone Fly, Grey Midge Adult, Henry's Fork Caddis Emerger.

Marvin Nolte

Marvin Nolte is one of America's finest and best-known flytyers. Born in 1947, he started tying in 1974. He became a professional flytyer in 1983 and specialises in fully dressed classic salmon flies. He tied all of the flies in the Grainger Collection: the largest collection of framed classic salmon flies in the world. Marvin has conducted courses and led flytying workshops in the US

Marvin Nolte spinning his magic to an admiring audience at the Fly Fair in Holland. *Rudy van Duijnhoven*

and in many European countries. He has contributed articles to several magazines including *Fly Fisherman* and *Fly Fishing and Fly Tying* (UK) and he is a regular columnist in *Fly Tyer* magazine. His book, *An Introduction to Aquatic Insects,* was published by the Federation of Fly Fishers. Marvin's flies have been used in several books, including *The Atlantic Salmon Fly,* by Judith Dunham; *Spinners,* by Sylvester Nemes and *Tying the Classic Salmon Fly,* edited by Michael D. Radencich. In 1995, Marvin received America's highest award for flytying, the Federation of Fly Fisher's Buz Buszek Memorial Fly Tying Award.

John Alevras CDC Steelhead

This attractive steelhead fly was shown to Marvin by John Alevras, of Colorado. The CDC Steelhead is more a style of fly than a specific pattern. It can be tied in many colour variations. The use of CDC in wet flies is not common in the US and Marvin is often asked at his demonstrations if the fly will float! These flies are fished as you would any steelhead or salmon wet fly. They have proved themselves many times on rivers in the American Northwest. These are three of the most effective patterns:

NO. 1

Hook: Partridge CS 10/2, Bartleet Supreme, size 1–6
Tail/hackle: Pheasant dyed black
Body: Copper diamond braid
CDC: Hot orange

NO. 2

Hook:	Partridge CS 10/2, Bartleet Supreme, size 1–6
Tail/hackle:	Golden pheasant breast
Body:	Gold diamond braid
CDC:	Purple

NO. 3

Hook:	Partridge CS 10/2, Bartleet Supreme, size 1–6
Tail/hackle:	Guinea fowl
Body:	Silver diamond braid
CDC:	Blue

Marven Nolte's CDC Steelhead Flies, variations of the same fly in different colours.

Nicolas Ragonneau

Nicolas is a specialist on the French rivers Dessoubre, Loue, Seine, Aube, Marne, Rognon and Bèze, for which he has designed some very useful flies. Although he is more than content to fish his beloved Dessoubre, he is sometimes tempted to travel abroad with friends to fish in Austria, Slovenia and England. Nicolas prefers the dry fly above all and uses natural materials almost exclusively for his flies, such as CDC, hare's ear, pheasant and certain cock hackles (Limousin or Pardo). Nicolas is addicted to CDC because the material is so soft and aerodynamic. He hates flies that twist the tippet after a few casts.

Besides fishing and tying innovative flies, Nicolas writes on the subject fly-fishing. With co-author Didier Ducloux, Nicolas recently published an impressive encyclopaedia, *Mouches de Pêche* (2001), containing dressings for 1,500 flies.

Nicolas Ragonneau fishing the Baca river in Slovenia in June 2001. A few moments after this photograph was taken he caught a superb grayling.

CDC flies by Nicolas Ragonneau. Clockwise from top left: Black Curse, Doigt de Rose, Saturday Night Sedge, Needle CDC, Bubble Caddis Emerger, Orange Lemon & Cinnamon.

1. BLACK CURSE

This is an imitation of the adult chironomid, which is notable for its mobile extended CDC body. Nicolas fishes it in lakes of the Massif Central and on the Lozère rivers.

Hook:	TMC 2487 or 2488, size 14–18
Thread:	Black 8/0
Extended body :	Grey/black CDC fibres wrapped with tying thread
Wing case/antennae:	White CDC
Thorax:	Grey/black CDC

2. DOIGT DE ROSE

A CDC Klinkhåmer variation that works well for trout and the 'lady of the stream'. It is a good pattern in low light conditions or in riffles. The name alludes to writings of the Greek poet, Homer.

Hook:	TMC 2488 (or 206 BL), size 10–18
Thread:	Grey 8/0
Abdomen:	Olive CDC
Thorax:	Blue dun CDC
Wing:	White CDC fibres
Hackle:	Pink CDC in a dubbing loop, parachute

3. BUBBLE CADDIS EMERGER

This is an imitation of a hatching caddis, with the characteristic bubble body and long antennae on either side.

Hook: TMC 900 BL, size 12–16

Thread: Grey 8/0

Under-

body: Pearl tinsel

Body: Olive or old yellow CDC fibres, tied from bend to eye in the form of a 'bubble'

Antennae: Dark grey CDC fibres

4. SOFT SEDGE

The Soft Sedge is one of Nicolas' favourites, which he uses as a searching pattern.

Hook: TMC 900 BL or 5210, size 10–16

Thread: Black or grey 8/0

Body: Tying thread

Wings: Two to six CDC feathers

Hackle: CDC fibres in a dubbing loop

5. SATURDAY NIGHT SEDGE

This is a variant of the Soft Sedge, tied with phosphorescent Flashabou on top and used when fishing the 'coup du soir' (evening twilight). Before fishing, the fly must be put under a white pocket torch to charge the luminous material.

Hook: TMC 900 BL or 5210, size 10—16

Thread: Black or grey 8/0

Body: Tying thread

Wings: Two to six CDC feathers, with several strands of phosphorescent Flashabou on top

Hackle: CDC fibres in a dubbing loop

6. TRICOLORE CDC AND ORANGE, LEMON & CINNAMON

A tribute to Henri Bresson's classic French pattern, the Tricolore, this CDC version is extraordinarily visible and a wonderful riffle fly. The colours can be changed according to preference and Nicolas ties versions in red, yellow and old yellow for rivers with dark riverbeds.

Hook: TMC 900 BL, size 10—18

Thread: Black 8/0

Hackles: Cream, old yellow, beige CDC hackled in a dubbing loop

7. NEEDLE CDC

An indispensable stonefly pattern for the rivers in Eastern France (Dessoubre, Loue, Doubs) in early spring. This is similar to the famous British needle fly imitation, but all in CDC.

Hook: TMC 900 BL, size 18–20
Thread: Orange-brown 8/0
Wings: Two small CDC feathers with flexible cement (Floo-Gloo)
Hackle: CDC in a dubbing loop

Philippe Boisson

Philippe is a well known flyfisherman in France, specialising in nymphs. He has a reputation as a 'pêche à vue' expert (i.e. fishing for 'seen' fish). He's also a good photographer and a creative tyer. Philippe is editor-in-chief of the French fishing magazine *Pêches Sportives*.

Philippe Boisson's Ombrelle, an unsual construction involving a kind of CDC parasol which is suspended above the fly by a piece of nylon.

The Ombrelle

The Ombrelle (meaning 'umbrella') is a remarkable fly distinguished by its 'detached wing' of CDC connected to the actual nymph by a few millimetres of monofilament. The Ombrelle does very well for Philippe who designed it especially for grayling but he finds it successful for trout too. The CDC toupé floats in the surface and performs the function of a wing. The Ombrelle is a highly visible fly and can be followed easily through streamy water.

The secret of the Ombrelle may lie in the fact that shy fish feed more confidently on food items hanging just below or in the surface rather than on those riding high on top of the surface.

Tying the Ombrelle is not very easy. There are two knots to be mastered for the assembly of the wing. The knot that connects the wing to the monofilament is a sliding knot. The second knot that connects the monofilament to the hook is just a normal one.

4. CDC CADDIS NO. 2

Hook: Daiichi 1310, size 14

Body: Condor dyed cinnamon (or substitute)

Wing: CDC feather dark brown tied at the end

Hackle: Hare mask fibres, natural

5. CDC CADDIS NO. 4

Hook: Daiichi 1310, size 14

Body: 12/0 thread - caramel

Wing: Hen mallard breast

Hackle: CDC fibres dark grey

6. CDC MISTIGRI

Hook: Daiichi 1310, size 14

Tail: Coq de León 'Flor d'Escobar' fibres

Body: Squirrel dubbing

Hackle: CDC fibres, dark grey

Jean-Louis Teyssié

Jean-Louis is lucky to live on the French Riviera, where the Alps cool their feet in the blue Mediterranean. He fishes mountain lakes, fast streams, canyon rivers, estuaries and in the sea all year round and ties flies for the whole range of his varied flyfishing. Jean-Louis has taken part in the international flytying contest in Norway and has won the best tyer award on three occasions. He writes articles on flyfishing and flytying in French, Italian, English and American magazines. His imitative patterns range from the impressionistic to the super-realistic. By mixing synthetic and classic materials Jean-Louis has developed a series of tube bodied flies incorporating CDC.

Jean-Louis Teyssié's Grey Spent Gnat.

1. MAY FLY SUBIMAGO

Hook:	TMC 103 BL, size 13
Thread:	Ultra fine black
Abdomen:	Olive CDC ephemera tube body (ref. JLT No. 20)
Tail:	Black cock feather
Thorax:	CDC brown fibres
Head:	CDC brown fibres
Legs:	Maxima nylon
Wings:	Olive and grey CDC
Eyes:	Maxima nylon, burned

2. GREY SPENT

Hook: TMC 103 BL, size 13

Thread: Ultra fine grey

Abdomen: Dun CDC ephemera tube body (ref. JLT No. 18)

Tail: Coq de León

Thorax: Peacock fibres

Head: Peacock fibres

Legs: Maxima nylon

Wings: Dun CDC

Eyes: Maxima nylon, burned

3. SULPHUR SPENT

Hook: TMC 103 BL, size17

Thread: Ultra fine yellow

Abdomen: Mixed olive CDC and yellow dubbing ephemera tube body (ref. JLT No. 22)

Tail: Yellow cock feather

Thorax: Yellow cock feather

Head: Yellow cock feather

Legs: Maxima nylon

Wings: Yellow and olive CDC

Eyes: Maxima nylon, burned

A superb imitation of the mayfly imago by Jean-Louis Teyssié, combining the extended body with CDC wings.

4. EPHEMERA EMERGER

Hook: TMC 103 BL, size19

Thread: Ultra fine black

Abdomen: Red ephemera tube body
            (ref. JLT No. 11)

Tail: Coq de León

Wing: Dun CDC

5. ANT

Hook: TMC 103BL, size13

Thread: Ultra fine black

Abdomen: Black diptera tube body
            (ref. JLT No. 1)

Thorax: CDC dun

Head: CDC dun

Antennae: Ultra fine black thread

Wings: Cock feather tips

6. MAY FLY IMAGO

Hook: TMC 103BL, size 11

Thread: Ultra fine black

Abdomen: May fly tube body (ref. JLT
            No. 24)

Tail: Cock

Thorax: Black foam

Head: Black foam

Legs: Maxima nylon

Wings: Mixed olive, dun and yellow
            CDC

Eyes: Maxima nylon, burned

The Ant, another of Jean-Louis Teyssié's CDC patterns which works well on his native rivers of southern France.

The Rumpled Leg Caddis.

Ryo Shimazaki's dramatic CDC Ballerina Dun.

Ryo Shimazaki

Ryo Shimazaki is an innovative fly designer and angling addict who lives in Tokyo. He is one of the new generation who have helped to develop flytying in recent times. Ryo is a frequent contributor to various flyfishing magazines. He works as a product development specialist with Tiemco Ltd.

CDC patterns by Ryo Shimazaki (left to right): Tome Dun, Floating Nymph, Hatching Dun.

Shimazaki's Caddis variations (left to right): Fluttering Caddis Adult, Rumpled Leg Caddis Adult, Caddis Adult.

1. RUMPLED LEG CADDIS ADULT

This fly can be fished either dead-drift or with a little movement given to it by the angler. Try to make the fly 'skitter' over the surface as the natural insects sometimes do.

Hook: TMC 200, size 10

Body: CDC Dubbing

Ribbing: Copper wire

Wing: Hen neck lined with CDC (using dou
            ble-sided tape)

Legs: Coq de León

2. CADDIS ADULT

Hook: TMC 902 BL, size 16

Body: Yellow monofilament thread

Wing: CDC

Legs: White splashed cock hackle

3. FLUTTERING CADDIS ADULT

Hook: TMC 100SP-BL, size 14

Wing: CDC

Legs: Blue dun cock hackle

4. CDC BALLERINA DUN

This was originally a Bill Logan fly pattern, but this version has a body of CDC.

Hook: TMC 205, size 12

Body: CDC

Wing: Deer hair

Legs: Coq de León

Tail: Pheasant tail

5. CDC HATCHING DUN

Aquatic insects are most vulnerable when their wings are drying out after hatching and prior to taking flight. The big wing of this dressing enhances the fluttering effect, especially if there is a breeze.

Hook: TMC 2488, size 14
Body: Partridge web and CDC dubbing
Wing: CDC
Shuck: Partridge web

6. TOME-DUN

The CDC wings are tied in thin profile thus creating a silhouette of real wings. 'Tome' is Ryo's nickname.

Hook: TMC 100 SP-BL, size 12
Body: Sulphur yellow dubbing
Wing: CDC
Legs: Cream cock hackle
Tail: Light dun cock hackle

7. FLOATING NYMPH

Suited for rather slow water. You can trim the wings to size if necessary while fishing.

Hook: TMC 106, size 14–16
Body: Cream dubbing
Wingcase and wing: CDC
Tail: Bronze mallard

Mitsugu Bizen

Mitsugu is a professional flytyer who lives at the foot of Mount Fuji. He has a house on a stream inhabited by highly educated and beautiful fish on which he tests his patterns. There is always a long waiting list for his flies.

1. HUMP & HANG

This pattern is in imitation of the floating emerger of the Pseudocloeon species. For extra durability, the wing case/indicator is constructed of both CDC and synthetic yarn.

Hook:	TMC 2499SP-BL, size 16–20
Thread:	Dark brown 8/0
Trailing shucks:	Emu feather
Body:	Yellow and ginger brown, mixed
Ribbing:	Fine gold wire
Wingcase and indicator:	Natural CDC with white Aero Dry Wing fine
Legs:	Natural dark dun cock hackle

2. ADAPTABLE DUN

This pattern is an imitation of the Japanese pale morning dun *Ephemerella rufa*. It was designed to represent a crippled dun that has failed to hatch, hanging helplessly in the surface.

Hook:	TMC 2499SP-BL, TMC 2488, size 16–22
Thread:	Dark brown 8/0
Tail:	Coq de León (Acerado)
Body:	Dyed orange peacock stripped quill
Thorax:	CDC fibre dubbing
Hackle:	Natural dark dun cock hackle
Indicator:	Natural CDC

3. FAR EAST TINY WINTER BLACK (DELTA WING STYLE)

This is an imitation of the tiny Nemouridae stonefly. These insects sometimes hatch on gusty late afternoons in early spring and late August. They are not very strong flyers and, in windy conditions, many get driven onto the surface of the water where the fish make a meal of them.

Hook: TMC 2499SP-BL or TMC 2488, size 16–20

Thread: Dark brown 8/0

Body: Japanese wild plant (Zenmai) cotton

Wing: CDC feather tip

Legs: Black cock hackle

Head: Same as body

4. UGLY GNAT

This is Mitsugu's best and most generally useful high-floating pattern. It could represent a micro caddis, a small ant or a chironomid. If used as a midge pattern, do not trim the palmered CDC.

Hook: TMC 100SP-BL or TMC 508, size 16–28

Thread: Dark brown 8/0

Body: Peacock herl

Body hackle: CDC

Nori Tashiro fishing the Sagae river in Japan.

Nori Tashiro

Nori is a respected and innovative fly designer. He and his brother, Tadayuki, conduct highly-rated research, even by the standard of specialist entomologists. Nori has published many articles on flyfishing and has developed over 300 patterns of flies as a result of his researches. Nori enjoys teaching others and he passes on his knowledge through the seminars and lectures he gives all over Japan.

1. RHYACOPHILA (SURFACE RUNNING PUPA)

This is a buoyant fly because of the CDC tied beneath the partridge legs. Even when this pupa is pulled under by drag, or when it is retrieved, it still floats well. Free-swimming sedge pupae can move quite quickly when they come up to hatch into adults and the fish take an active interest in them. To fish this pattern, you should cast downstream or down and across. By controlling the fly, you should aim to retrieve your pupa at a similar speed as the natural pupa moves.

Hook: TMC 2312, size 16–18
Thread: Uni thread olive 8/0
Body: Tashiro RSC dub - No. 06
Thorax: Tashiro RSC dub - No.06
Wing case: Black duck quill
Legs: Dun CDC and brown partridge
Antennae: Wood duck
Eyes: Burned monofilament

2. CHEUMATOPSYCHE (FLAP ADULT)

'I once faced a super-migration of Cheumatopsyche on Montana's Missouri River in August. I was almost snowed under by caddis. This imitation of the flying adult fly is very effective when adult caddis flies are fluttering over the surface in the course of migration, or drifting down stream after egg-laying.'

Hook: TMC 900BL, size 18–20
Thread: Uni thread grey 8/0
Body: Tashiro RSC dub - No.03
Wing: CDC khaki
Hackle: Grizzly
Antennae: Wood duck

3. BRACHYCENTRUS ADULT (LOOP WING)

'The wings of the caddis adult are covered by cilia. Caddis fold their wings when they are moving on the surface, diving and swimming. CDC is a very effective material for tying loop wings.'

Hook: TMC 900BL, size 16–18
Thread: Uni thread grey 8/0
Body: Tashiro RSC dub - No.12
Wing: CDC khaki
Hackle: Cree
Antennae: Wood duck

4. DIPTERA ADULT (LOOP WING)

An imitation of a small adult dipteran, drifting on the surface with folded wings. An artificial that is one or two sizes larger than the natural insect might even represent a cluster. The palmered hackle could imitate the tangled legs of a couple of adults.

Hook: TMC 100BL, size 20–24
Thread: Ultra fine thread black 12/0
Body: Black super fine dub
Wing: CDC dun
Hackle: Grizzly

5. BAETIS TWO IN ONE

Called the 'Two in One' because this fly can be used as both a dun and spinner pattern. The CDC feathers give both styles a soft appearance which is good for light presentation.

Hook: TMC 900BL, size 18—20
Thread: Olive grey ultra fine thread 12/0
Body: Brown olive super fine dub
Thorax: Same as body
Wing: CDC dun
Hackle: Medium dun
Tail: Coq de León

Five patterns by Nori Tashiro (clockwise from top left): Rhyacophila, Cheumatopsyche, and Brachycentrus Adult, Baetis 'two in one', and Diptera Adult.

'I can truthfully say that in what approaches fifty years of fly fishing and tying flies few, if any, natural materials I have tried can equal cul de canard in producing the life-giving effect that has become so important on hard-fished waters.'

René Harrop in John Roberts' *The World's Best Trout Flies* (1994)

There is a growing pressure on fishing waters worldwide and things aren't likely to get any better. Waters that are easily accessible get overcrowded and heavily fished. While a few anglers have the luxury of departing for more remote areas, the ones who stick to their home waters find the fishing gets harder.

As fishing pressure increases and the fish see more and more of the angler's offerings, they become increasingly educated. This is especially so where catch-and release is practised, since the fish get a chance to learn from any mistakes! As the fish become more educated and difficult, the flyfisher requires better and more subtle imitations. CDC patterns have made a great contribution in this regard: helping flyfishers meet the challenge of increasingly difficult fishing for more sophisticated fish.

CDC dry flies

The range of effective CDC dry flies and emergers covers everything from the smallest Wee Whisper (see page 102) to a huge Rugged Caddis (see page 69). Every pattern has its own particular application and requires an appropriate fishing style to get the best from it. That notwithstanding, it is possible to give some general advice on fishing with CDC dry flies and emergers.

To improve buoyancy, it helps to treat fly bodies (not the CDC wings!) with a tiny amount of Marc Petitjean's CDC Oil. After catching a fish, rinse the fly thoroughly in the water to remove dirt and fish slime. Dry the fly with amadou or tissue paper and make a few brisk false casts to finish the job. Specialist desiccant preparations like Tiemco's Shimazaki Dry Shake seem to dry flies even better.

Over the years I've taken to changing flies rather frequently; the very act of changing them gives me a chance to pause and decide how to proceed. Sometimes I might just tie on a fresh version of the same fly, on other occasions I will change to a different pattern altogether. In my pre-CDC period I regularly fished on with the same fly for hours on end. In those days I didn't usually change my fly until I noticed that strikes decreased or failed to come at all. I can assure you that seldom occurs now. In recent years, I've been changing flies much more frequently and in doing so I have gained a deeper understanding of fly selection. Another improvement to my catch rate has come from changing fly sizes regularly. A fresh fly and a different pattern or size can really make all the difference.

Fishing CDC flies

Handle CDC dries and emergers with care. Don't bang the fly down hard when you make your delivery cast, as this could drown the fly at the outset. Present the fly as gently and accurately as possible. Short drifts enable you to lift off line, leader and fly softly and quickly and it will also help to keep the fly dry. Long drifts, on the other hand, reduce line control and often result in your fragile CDC fly being dragged under water so that it will need to be dried or replaced.

Control your drifts and when lifting off, raise the rod and tease the line from the water, before lifting off quickly. The more cleanly one can pluck the fly from the surface, the longer it will stay dry.

If a CDC fly is merely pulled under by the current, it shouldn't really get soaked. Normally, it pops up again after a few yards and floats on happily. A dry CDC fly pulled under water by the current looks like a big air bubble.

Leader arrangement

Changing flies frequently demands an appropriate leader structure. Tippets get a little bit shorter every time a fly is changed. While fishing for salmon in Norway with Hans van Klinken, several years ago, he taught me a simple and obvious principle: wherever possible, avoid superfluous knots. Since then I have adopted his leader system. Hans uses a braided leader, slipped over the fly line and attached securely by a close thread whipping coated with waterproof glue. To the little loop connection at the thin end of the braid, he attaches a tippet of desired length and diameter using either a loop-to-loop connection, or a tucked half blood knot. Tippets can easily be replaced when needed. The system is simple, effective and safe.

Sub surface fishing

CDC fibres have plenty of action. Since I am addicted to using wet flies which have action, CDC patterns meet this criterion. Sub-surface fly fishing can be very rewarding on both still waters and rivers, since this is where the fish do most of their feeding. But fishing nymphs and streamers can be a rather uncertain business, for, in most cases, it is impossible to see how and where exactly the fly is moving. Nevertheless, it is of prime importance to fish the nymph in a natural way. Fish can invariably see clearly what our flies look like and how they 'behave' under water. If a dead drift is required, it is important that your fly doesn't drift slower or faster than the current as this will alert the fish that something is amiss. But even moving at same speed as the current, soft materials like CDC still has movement of its own and this gives the fly the appearance of being alive. It is, however, nearly impossible to control the sub-surface fly with any certainty. There are so many potential influences on the movement of the fly and leader; one simply can't know everything that is happening down there.

On certain occasions it is necessary to fish a nymph very deep and close to the bottom and this poses all kinds of practical difficulties to the flyfisher. Fish that are hugging the bottom are rarely inclined to move up in the water to intercept a fly and we must therefore fish our flies down at their level to be successful. Cover the holding area thoroughly with enough casts to make sure that the fish has seen the fly. When retrieving after a drift, always allow the fly to be taken away downstream of the fish by the current before quietly lifting off well behind any possible lies.

L NYMPH

Hook:	TMC 200, size 8-16 with lead wire windings
Thread:	Brown 8/0
Rib:	Copper wire
Body:	Brown CDC dubbing
Wing case:	Mottled turkey feather
Thorax:	Brown rabbit fur and CDC fibres (in dubbing loop)

1. Wrap lead wire around the hook shank and secure with thread and cement.

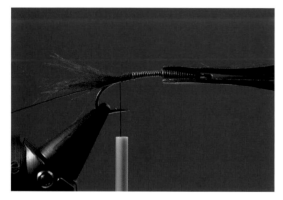

2. Take the thread to a position above the hook barb and tie in a tail of CDC fibres of about half the length of the hook shank. Tie in a length of copper wire.

3. Spin a thin 'noodle' of brown CDC dubbing onto the thread and wind an abdomen for approximately two-thirds of the shank.

4. Rib with the copper wire, secure and trim off

5. Tie in a sliver of the mottled turkey feather for the wingcase. Form a dubbing loop at the same point, into which insert some brown rabbit fur and, at the end of the loop, some CDC fibres (with the help of a paper clamp).

6. Carefully twist the loop and wind the thorax with it. Clip off the fibres on top and on the underside of the thorax.

7. Pull the turkey wing case material forward and over the top of the thorax. Tie off and trim the excess.

8. Whip finish and lacquer head and wing case.

CDC dry flies, semi dry flies, nymphs and streamers have improved my catch rates considerably. Even where fishing pressure is high, or the fish very selective, a small and sparsely tied CDC fly has often provided the remedy. Patterns tied with this extraordinary material have revolutionised my own flyfishing. If you have never fished CDC flies before, I strongly advise you to give them a try. I am confident you won't be disappointed. Tight lines!

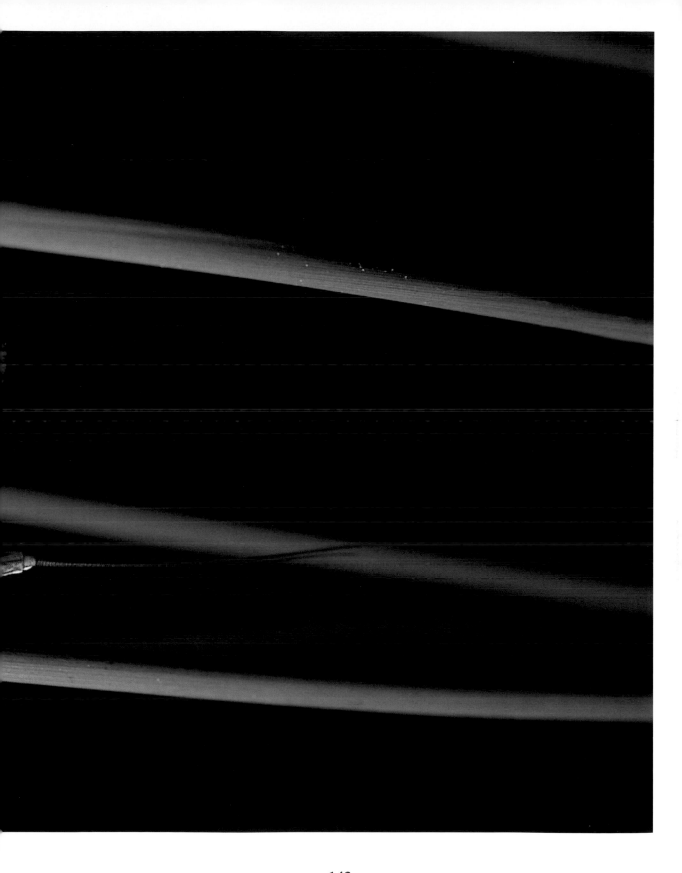

Addresses of Suppliers

Giorgio Benecchi's Products
Via Giotto 279
41100 Modena
Italy

Henri Bresson
Magasin Plein Air
32, Rue Georges-Genoux
70000 Vesoul
France

Mouches Devaux Champagnole
BP 267 – 01202 Bellegarde Valserine Cedex
France

House of Harrop
P.O. Box 491
St. Anthony, Idaho 83445
United States of America

Petitjean Fishing Equipment SA
Route J. Chaley 52
CH- Fribourg
Switzerland
www.petitjean.com

Traun River Products
Hauptstraße 4
D-83313 Siegsdorf
Germany

E. Veniard LTD.
138 Northwood Road
Thornton Heath
Surrey
England CR7 8YG

Bibliography

From the 1970s

Jules Rindlisbacher - *Der praktische Fliegenfischer* Zürich, 1970
  First publication discussing CDC flies.
A. Courtney Williams - *A Dictionary of Trout Flies*, London, 1973
  First English publication containing a CDC fly, the 'Duck and Cock dun' sent by Yves Rameaux.
Dr. Jean-Paul Pequegnot - *Répertoire des Mouches Artificielles Françaises*, 1975
  Containing general information on CDC feathers, origin of the fly in the Swiss section of the Jura and variations of Aimé Devaux and Henri Bresson.
Jean-Paul Metz - Vorbild und Nachahmung, *Der Fliegenfischer* 4, 1975, p. 22-24
  On the Blue Winged Olive and imitating it with CDC flies and other imitations.
Dr. Jean-Paul Metz, Horst Kretschmer and Rudi Rubel -
Zwanzig Fliegenmuster reichen aus! Nürnberg, 1977.
  First publication ever to explain how the traditional Swiss CDC pattern is tied.
Günther Fröhlich - Über den Umgang mit Mimosen, Der Fliegenfischer 29, 1979, p. 32-33
  A pioneering article on the CDC feather as a tying material.

After 1980

  The above reports marked the beginning of a large flow of interesting
  publications that contributed to the increasing interest for CDC. Here is a selection of them:
Dr. Klaus von Bredow - Das große Buch vom Fliegenbinden, Zürich, 1981
Kees Ketting - Een hand vol vliegen, 1983
Dr. Bozidar Volj_ - Fratnikova Puhovka Ribi_ Sept. 1983, p. 262-263
Marjan Fratnik - Die F.F.F. Der Fliegenfischer 54, 1984 , p. 28-29
Gerhard Laible - Die Kombinierte Elementbehechelung, Der Fliegenfischer 61, 1985, p.28-29
Gerhard Laible - In meiner Technik: Die Danica – Sequenz,
  Der Fliegenfischer 65, 1986, p.36-39
Gerhard Laible - Vom Cul de Canard articles, starting in *Der Fliegenfischer* 77, 1988
Dr. Jean-Paul Pequegnot - *French Fishing Flies*, New York, 1987
René Harrop - Cul de Canard Flies, *Fly Fisherman*, July, 1991 p.48-51/59
Gerhard Laible - *CDC Flies*, Siegsdorf, 1993
Darrel Martin - *Micropatterns*, Shrewsbury, 1994
John Roberts - *The World's Best Trout Flies*, London, 1994
Dr. Jean-Paul Pequegnot - *L'Art de la Pêche a la Mouche Sèche*, Besançon, 1996
Charles Richter - La belle et véritable histoire du Cul-de-Canard *Pêche Mouche* 5, 1997
Malcolm Greenhalgh & Denys Ovenden - *The Complete Fly-Fisher's Handbook*, London, 1998
Didier Ducloux & Nicolas Ragonneau - *Mouches de Pêche, L'encyclopédie*, Losange, 2001

Index

155